# Lil Bit of Swansboro with Captain Joe Webb

## Chad Hollamon

Cushing Publishing
www.cushingpublishing.com

Captain Joe Webb and Chad Hollamon

Copyright @2023 Chad Hollamon
ISBN: 979-8-9889575-0-8

Cushing Publishing
P.O. Box 38
Middlesex, NC 27557

Editor Julia Fisher
Publisher Cushing Publishing
Photos from NC Archives, Chad Hollamon, Joe Webb,
Jeremy Denning, Melissa Webb, Joe Rhue, and Billy
Parkin unless otherwise noted.

# Acknowledgements

Many residents of Swansboro had a hand in making this journey possible. Norman Wells, Bobby Wells, Josh Wells, Susan Casper, Charles Teachey, Rob Koraly, Darren Tupper, Gloria Sanders, Melissa Webb, Jim Corbette, Diane Williams, Jack Dudley, Jeremy Denning, Joe Rhue and the Historical Society of Swansboro. Each were instrumental to the contents and context of this book. Opening up your homes and places of businesses allowed me to find out more about your beautiful hometown. I can call many of you my new friends. Thank you immensely for the opportunity.

# Table of Contents

# PROLOGUE
## A GLIMPSE OF THE PAST
## AUGUST 1947
## SWANSBORO, NORTH CAROLINA

For six-year-old Joe, the summer morning started as a typical day in this eastern North Carolina coastal town. He woke up on the floor, sweating due to the overnight humidity and having no air-conditioner in the small one-story house. After standing up, Joe stretched his arms over his head to get a kink out of his neck. The boy was both anxious and excited to begin the day. The waterfront in this small fishing village always seemed to be an adventure. If there was anything for a six-year-old boy to get into, Joe would find it and dive in feet first.

Along the way to the kitchen, floorboards creaked under each footstep. The house was empty of occupants. Joe's parents Horace and Katherine Webb had already left for work at their grocery store before the sun came up. Once in the cozy kitchen, Joe pushed a bar stool close to the food cupboards. Katherine or Mrs. Kitty as everyone called her, supposedly hid the sugar from her son but Joe had a nose for its whereabouts. Climbing the chest-high stool was no easy feat. However, the six-year-old boy did just that and then stood on his tippy toes to locate the bowl of sugar hidden behind a bag of flour. With a small spoon, Joe fished a few scoops into his mouth before having his fill. Neatly, he returned the bowl to its hiding place before jumping down. After sliding the stool to its original position, Joe would be ready to explore the world he knew.

Joe's attire would consist of nothing more than a pair of shorts. He didn't even bother wearing a pair of shoes or sandals, his feet calloused from the countless miles he trekked across the uneven downtown Swansboro streets and roads. With some coins in one front pocket and a set of shooting marbles in the opposite one, Joe marched out of the quaint house on the corner of 5th and Main Street. Without locking the door behind him, Joe peered out onto the White Oak River, less than a hundred yards directly in front of him. The bright sun gleamed off the water as Joe made a right turn down Main Street.

To relieve himself of the dangling change in his pocket, Joe's first stop would be Mr. Rigg's Store two blocks down from his house. Dr. Corbett, the town doctor had his office in the same building as the busy store where men stood out front, simply to hang out. Joe was greeted by them all before entering the Rigg's Store. Joe smelled rubbing alcohol as soon as he came into the establishment. Mr. Riggs was known to wash his hands constantly with the solution. As Joe walked the aisles, he saw huge blocks of cheese that had to weigh ten pounds apiece. Joe considered purchasing some of that same cheese, but he craved sugar, so he made his way to the candy section. The whole time Joe searched for his candy of choice, Mr.

Riggs stocked the shelves, limping each time he moved on the wooden floors. An old injury caused him to favor one leg over the other.

Standing at the cash register with a bottle of Pepsi and a pack of M&M's laying on the counter, Joe laid down the change he produced from his pocket.

Mr. Riggs made his way to the young boy and eyed him curiously as he slid the coins in his hand, "You going to do that outside, Joe?" he asked.

Joe found amusement by putting the candy M&M's in the bottle. When doing so, a chemical reaction forced some of the liquid to spew out like an erupting volcano, often making a mess. Mr. Riggs had to clean up after Joe on more than one occasion.

Joe smiled and assured the owner, "Yes sir. I'll do it on the sidewalk."

After stepping outside, Joe proceeded with his juvenile ritual. After placing the M&M's in the bottle, the brown liquid oozed out, causing Joe to laugh at himself. The men standing nearby egged on the six-year-old boy. Joe drank the rest of the contents in one long gulp, then threw his trash away in a large can by the street. Sugar was the last thing Joe needed. He was already known as the boy that couldn't sit still. Back in those days, they didn't have the term 'ADHD,' nor was there a diagnosis for the hyperactive disorder. However, that is exactly what Joe's behaviors suggested.

Even from that early age, he was always into something. If he was forced to sit down, Joe fidgeted his feet and hands. The boy, like I said, couldn't sit still. Being fidgety would remain with Joe for the rest of his long life and would land him into all kinds of mischief. That same pent-up energy would also make him the life of the party in later years.

Noontime would be hours away, but the sweltering heat was already an undeniable force. Joe continued down Main Street. Walking at a brisk pace, in less than a minute Joe could see where the White Oak River met the inlets connecting to the Atlantic Ocean – like crooked fingers with uninhabited islands, as far as the eyes could see. Fishing vessels, freight boats, and the occasional line boat came and went from the docks; the clattering of equipment and fishing poles flapping about on the vessels from the light southwesterly wind. Men could be heard yelling back and forth. What might seem to be chaos to the average person, would be a beautifully orchestrated symphony to Joe.

Once Joe made it to the waterfront, residents there referred to the six-year-old boy by his first name. Everyone knew the youngster and Joe made it a point to know everyone by name. In fact, with Swansboro's population less than five-hundred people in 1947, everyone knew everyone. It was a tight-knit community. Joe waved at Jesse Moore, owner, and operator of the charter boat 'The Ranger.' There was also Captain Charlie, Ed Foster, Thomas Parkin, Lee Jones, and Captain Aman, all men whose lives were dedicated to the water.

There were no strangers or tourists like this community would see in later years.

Sure, fishermen visited from nearby towns like Morehead City, New Bern, and Jacksonville but they came here mostly for work. Only a handful of families called this sleepy village home. Everything seemed to be in perfect harmony, no matter the hardships this era might've brought. Life was yet to be complicated in this part of the world. Most men either built houses and boats, farmed, or fished. The women also pulled their weight. They were schoolteachers and homemakers that did everything to make this community come together as one, including helping in the fields during harvest time and assisting the fishermen at peak seasons.

Between docks, Joe eavesdropped on the fishermen's conversations. There was a lot of buzz going on about one of their own being missing for over a week. A good-natured man but a heavy drinker named Jimmy Canady disappeared out of thin air. He was last seen near his fish house on the waterfront that he leased from Tyre Moore. There was only speculation as to his whereabouts. Some locals said, "he went out on his boat and never returned,". Some last saw him drinking booze on the docks. Last but not least, someone claimed "he ran off to Wilmington", some seventy miles away. One thing's for sure, no one seemed to know where Jimmy Canady was at. His presence was missed.

Six-year-old Joe fumbled with the marbles in his pocket as he aimlessly wandered between docks. Brand new fishing vessels returned from the ocean, full of Seabass, Red Drum, and other fish they caught while bottom fishing. One of the last remaining freight boats slowly maneuvered its way through the inlets, full of household goods. Downtown Swansboro was the epicenter of the planet to Joe. Its liveliness and vibrancy lit up his eyes. He was unaware of a world outside of here. He didn't know Swansboro had its first bridges built a few years before he was born. Before that, the town was cut off from nearby towns. One had to travel by boat to get to places like New Bern, Beaufort, or Morehead City. Life during this time would be lived without television and technology. One only knew what was in front of them.

Swansboro during the 1940s was a mix of disappearing sawmills, busy fish factories, small tobacco farms, and boat-building shops, while commercial fishing came to employ most of the locals. Quick access to the deep waters of the Atlantic Ocean made this area ideal for both inshore and offshore fishing. There were numerous shrimp boats, charter boats, party boats, and small skiffs dotting the docks of the waterfront. The fish primarily brought everyone together. So much so that the town would acquire the nickname, 'Friendly City by the Sea.' Vehicle bumper stickers would also soon appear that read, 'Welcome to Swansboro, N.C., 2,000 Population, 20,000,000 Fish,' even though the general population was a third of that. People of Swansboro were proud to call this small community home, and people that lived nearby loved to visit this quaint village.

Before fishing took over, sawmills kept the majority of the men of Swansboro working. It was said that nearly fifty percent of the locals in the early 1900s worked at the Prettyman Mill, Swindell Mill, Interstate Cooperage Company, White Oak River Corporation, or Swansboro Land and Lumber Company. The White Oak River was considered the highway of the sea. During that era, instead of seeing fishing vessels like in later years, you would see steam-powered tugboats towing rafts loaded down with logs to the various mills in the area. By the 1920s timber became severely outsourced, meaning sawmills would be replaced by other industries like fishing and boat building, thus ending a noteworthy period for the town of Swansboro and the immediate area.

After hearing more chatter about the disappearance of Jimmy Canady, Joe decided to head over to Mr. Canady's fish house to check things out himself. He took Front Street, passing multiple downtown establishments like the Swansboro Ice Plant owned by Steve Milstead, Swan Café owned by Mabel Gerock, and his dad's store called H.B. Webb Grocery. People came downtown to work and to purchase goods. It was also a place where some of the locals 'people watched.' There was an old saying which citizens used during this time: 'down the street'. When an individual might have been asked where they were going, the person would answer, 'down the street.' Down the street was a vague term for hanging out on Front Street or on the docks.

Joe continued down Front Street with some pep in his step. Harry B. Moore walked in the opposite direction of Joe, on his way to the building he worked out of. Mr. Moore was a financier, who loaned money to local farmers and anyone in need of financial assistance. There was another Harry Moore around town, but his middle name started with an M. Harry M. Moore was a captain on a boat called Sonny Boy.

Wearing a sharp suit, Harry B. Moore greeted Joe, "Morning."

"Good morning, Mr. Moore, going to be hot today, ain't it," said Joe.

"Looks like it. Those feet are gonna melt." Replied Mr. Moore.

Joe looked down at his bare feet and said, "That ought to be a sight".

Joe cut back to the other side of the street where the Canady Fish House sat between Rhue's Hardware store and the Littleton Fish House. Jimmy Canady's building seemed deserted other than a few small boats tied up nearby and fishing nets hung to dry. Not seeing much activity, Joe headed towards the Casper property where a marina had recently been built on top of what was once Swansboro Land and Lumber Company. Joe frequently met his acquaintances there, including his good friend W.T. Casper, for a game of marbles. He took a right down Church Street and then immediately hung a left on Water Street. His pace slowed down when coming up on Poor Man's Hole. Poor Man's Hole was where Isiah Willis and Monte Hill built affordable boats.

Joe stared at what the two builders were able to assemble. Each boat was handcrafted. Some were so big or intricate, Joe didn't have an idea of how they even floated on the water. He did know that he was going to have a boat of his own, on the waterfront one day. Fishing and everything that came with it was in Joe's blood.

Approaching Broad Street and Casper's Marina, bustling activity could be seen around the gas pumps that carried Shell gasoline. Fishermen and dockhands eyed Joe but didn't give him a second glance. He would be a fixture to the marina, often referred to as Horace's boy or the marina owner's grandson's friend. Joe took to the shoreline and peered down at the murky water. Small fish could be seen in their aquatic habitat. The six-year-old could name each species with ease. Life on the water came naturally to him.

Old man Joe Casper himself stood at the end of one dock, winding a rope around his elbow and palm. Mr. Casper noticed Joe and motioned for him to come over to him. An obedient Joe strolled over to him, staring at how the man wrapped the rope up in a small bundle.

Mr. Casper asked, "You and W.T. going swimming?"

"No sir. We fixin' to shoot some marbles," Joe said.

"That's fine. Two things. Ya'll watch out for boats when you swim. One or both of you is going to get killed. The second thing is, no sparklers are to be lit up near here. I don't care if it's someone's birthday. Those gas tanks are full. If one of them catches fire, someone is going to get hurt. And bad. No sparklers. Understand," Mr. Casper said.

"Yes sir," Joe replied, even though he would often be mischievous.

"Now, how is your dad and Mrs. Kitty?" Mr. Casper asked.

Before Joe could answer, he pointed to an

object out in the shallow water. It appeared to be a small abandoned dingy. Mr. Casper saw it at that point and then yelled out to some men standing near the gas pumps behind him, "Someone go inside and call the fire department! The rest of you come over here!"

The men crowded around Joe and old man Casper. Joe knew them all, including W.T.'s dad named Bill. Bill Casper owned the 'Billy Jean,' a prominent boat in these waters. Joe got pushed further to the back as the men inspected the dingy. The object drifted closer and closer to them. That's when Joe saw the human features on the so-called dingy. Even though it had human features, it was bloated twice the size of any man Joe had ever seen. Joe noticed crabs and other creatures coming out of crevices. Men quickly jumped into the water. Suddenly, the sirens of the town's new firetruck could be heard in the near distance. Upon closer look, Joe registered that it wasn't a dingy. It was that of a middle-aged man.

The mystery of Jimmy Canady's disappearance ended that hot summer morning. Mr. Canady's body washed up just a few blocks from his beloved fish house. He had drowned and it would be Joe and old man Casper to be the first ones to see him in twelve days. The men pulled the body out of the water. They backed the six-year-old up, but Joe could still see the bloated dead body. The fire department arrived and took over.

Seeing the disfigured dead body would have a traumatic effect on Joe. For the ensuing weeks after this incident, Joe couldn't sleep by himself.

He either slept with his mom or his nana Aida. The sight of Jimmy Canady's body would be something Joe would never forget. It would be a story Joe came to tell over and over during his long lifetime. It only added to the life experiences he would encounter in the quaint little town of Swansboro, North Carolina.

# INTRODUCTION
## MAY 2022
## SWANSBORO, NORTH CAROLINA

An hour or thereabout after the sun had come up on this late spring morning, three loved ones and I sat in the living room of a tiny old cottage in the historic downtown district. My mom (Candy) and my girlfriend (Melissa) occupied the couch. The six-year-old boy you just read about is now eighty-year-old Captain Joe Webb. Both he and I sat in club chairs on opposite sides of the couch, the flat-screen TV showing the latest news. Melissa and I had just woken up when mom and her dear friend Captain Joe stopped by in the middle of their early morning walk.

During the idle talk about how each of us was going to fulfill our day, bombs and live ammunition could be heard in the near distance. The noises are common in this area. The military, especially that of the marines, practices, and trains at Camp Lejeune in Jacksonville, some fifteen miles away. Sometimes they even drop bombs on Brown Island, a barrier island three miles from the heart of Swansboro. Tourists and newcomers often believe the bombs to be thunder, which is understandable. The vibrations can often rock the foundations of houses and shake windowpanes, to the point where one may think the glass will shatter. You get used to it after you spend some time here. So much so that you tend to ignore it because of the bombs and live ammunition being a frequent occurrence.

The locals have dubbed the training as, 'the sounds of freedom,' due to the military practicing warfare to keep us Americans safe from those countries possibly intending harm on our much-loved freedom. The blasts are welcomed by most and not seen as a nuisance. I take pride in living close to so many active and non-active military men and women. Every single day numerous military planes and helicopters fly overhead from nearby Camp Lejeune, Camp Davis, Bogue Airfield, Cherry Point Marine Air Corps Station, and Seymour Johnson Air Force Base. The bombs, live ammunition, planes, and helicopters are added features to this scenic area along the Crystal Coast, also known as the Southern Outer Banks of North Carolina.

Captain Joe Webb sat there studying the interior of the old house Melissa rented at 206 Water Street. He started telling us facts about the house we were in and recalled different families like Hubert and Sally Dennis that once called it home. Joe regularly did this. When it came to knowing anything or anybody about Swansboro, he was like a walking encyclopedia. Guess any eighty-year-old that's born and raised in a small town will know its history, while having memories of every street and house around. Joe knew Swansboro and the waters around it like the proverbial 'back of his hand.' He'd find his way around on the streets or waterways blindfolded.

Joe is widely known as a captain because he ran a charter fishing business for over fifty years. His current boat, the 'Billy Anna II,' is a mainstay in downtown Swansboro. For decades, the Billy Anna II has withstood hurricanes, numerous powerful storms, lightning strikes, brisk winters, and thousands of miles out in the Atlantic Ocean. If there are fish in these waters, Captain Joe Webb knows where to find and catch them. I've had the honor of being out on the Billy Anna II on numerous occasions. He has a multitude of favorite spots in the ocean to catch certain species of fish. Other local fishermen have been known to follow him in order to land the big fish. But most of the time, it's not only where to find the fish, it's knowing what bait to use and what time of day to catch them. Joe has had the recipe for decades to catch any fish in these waters.

Joe may not be world renowned, but here in good old Swansboro and other fishing villages in North Carolina, thousands of people know him personally, or the legendary stories told about him. Swansboro has been his life. Not even the current mayor gets as much recognition as Joe. If I could describe Joe in two words it would be; Ernest Hemingway. From his white beard, mannerisms, and colloquies, he'd win any Hemingway look-alike contest. From personal experience and other accounts, he'd more than likely drink Ernest Hemingway under the table. The man may know fish, but he can also drink like one too and I'll not shy away from sharing some of those stories with you.

As Joe sat in the club chair crossing his legs in his trademark way, he continued telling us story after story about different eras of Swansboro. He could recall names and events like no one around. One story would lead to another story, making you feel like you know the person or people he's talking about. Joe can put you in the story as if you are there. Great story tellers can do that. They can make you laugh. They can make you cry. They can often make you cringe.

Candy commented, "Joe, with all the stories you have, you should write a book."

Joe shrugged the suggestion off. I've heard Candy say that to him countless times over the past twenty-five years or so. Joe might be a Hemingway look-alike, but he couldn't tell one story without bouncing around to another. While he's sharp for any man twenty years younger, and he has fascinating stories he can ramble from one to another making him difficult to keep up with. He will admit this is due to his short attention span.

Joe has lived a colorful life with numerous adventures. Reminds me of an old Dos Equis beer commercial. The campaign aired a greying wise man as, 'The Most Interesting Man in the World.' Joe fits that mold.

Joe rambled on. However, Melissa stopped him when he came to the end of another story. She looked at me and said, "Chad, you should write the book with Joe."

"Me?" I questioned.

Then it came to me as to why Melissa would suggest this. See, I had recently written a book titled, 'Cries for Carteret.' Its release date was just a few short months away. I knew of the hard work it took to write a book. It also took years of writing to hone my craft about my own life experiences and not someone else's. But saying that, I also knew of the reward when finally completing a book or screenplay. The wind of writing another book had lifted my sails. I sat there contemplating the suggestion of my girlfriend.

Candy interjected with excitement, "That's a great idea!"

"Let me think about it," I answered both of them.

As the four of us sat there, I replayed their words in my mind. My thoughts went into overdrive envisioning a complete book about some of the history of Swansboro including Captain Joe Webb. Back and forth I went with ideas and possibilities. I asked myself 'How can I honor this man and his stories with Swansboro as my backdrop?'

I blurted out, 'Lil Bit of Swansboro with Captain Joe Webb!' That's what I'm going to call it. What do you think?"

I could tell that I had won everyone's approval. I turned to Joe, "I can start in a few months, You up for it?"

"Boy, when I was born, the whole town of Swansboro closed down," Joe answered the way he knew how with slick and quick-witted comebacks.

Bombs could still be heard in the near distance. 'BOOM!' 'BOOM!' As each one went off I couldn't wait to get started writing this book at the end of summer. Three things kept on echoing in my head; Captain Joe Webb. Swansboro. History. I smiled, realizing how this book would come together. I smiled, understanding the task ahead of me. I smiled, seeing my mom's face. After all these years, her suggestions were coming to fruition.

*Candy and Captain Joe Webb circa 1995*

# CHAPTER ONE
# AN EXPERIENCE LIKE NO OTHER

I'm sorry. I didn't get a chance to formally introduce myself. My name is Chad Hollamon. Back in 1993, my parents moved our family from Goldsboro, North Carolina, a small city between the state capitol in Raleigh and the seaside village of Swansboro. We made our new home in the coastal community of Emerald Isle, a barrier island, five miles north of Swansboro. Though the townships are close in proximity, they couldn't be any more different in terms of culture and history.

Emerald Isle pretty much remained a remote and uninhabited island until the 1950s. Yes, the Algonquin Indians camped there in earlier centuries, but it was only a beautiful beach full of trees and lush vegetation until early in the twentieth century when the Coast Guard built a station there overlooking Bogue Inlet. Emerald Isle didn't even have its first bridge until the 1970s. In the present day there are no historic buildings there, only older cottages, mobile homes, and million-dollar houses popping up left and right.

Anyhow, Emerald Isle is a typical beach town. Thousands of tourists visit in the summer months. However, it does slow down considerably between Labor Day and Memorial Day weekend. Other small towns surrounding Emerald Isle are

Beaufort, Salter Path, Cape Carteret, Cedar Point, Atlantic Beach, Morehead City, and Harker's Island. Each town is unique in its way. When driving through the area, you don't need a road sign to tell you that you are exiting one community or entering another one. The numerous bridges and various types of trees will let you know that you're in a different place. Some places in Onslow and Carteret Counties feel like you are in a different country altogether. The area is beautiful in every sense of the word.

Not long after moving to Emerald Isle, my parents went through a divorce. My brother, Brad, and I remained with my father in Emerald Isle. Mom moved in with her new boyfriend, none other than Captain Joe Webb in Swansboro. Joe lived in a house directly beside the one he grew up in. Joe's mother, Mrs. Kitty was in her eighties at the time and had remained in the same house since the 1930s, so in essence, they were neighbors. I vividly remember going to check on Mrs. Kitty with my mom or Joe. Mrs. Kitty was a small, fragile woman with a kind heart and a time-clocked appetite. She always ate lunch by 12:30 PM. If no one brought her food, she would call Joe immediately.

Captain Joe seemed to be an odd fit for mom. They met at The Yacht Club, kind of a dive bar at the time but a favorite watering hole for the Swansboro locals in the 1990s. The Yacht Club itself lay on a small island between the two Swansboro bridges, connecting Onslow County to Carteret County. Clyde Phillip's Seafood shared the island with the popular club. Large shrimp boats of yesteryear remain docked behind Clyde Phillip's Seafood, giving the area a postcard look when the sun sets in the evenings.

Joe was nearly twenty years older than my mom when they met, with an already greying head of hair and beard. Didn't add up, but mom seemed legitimately happy with him. I was probably a little cold to Joe initially. But over the first six months, the man grew on me. When visiting the fisherman's house, it fascinated me to see all these old photos hanging on the walls, some dating back to the early 1900s. As I stared at one, Joe spoke from behind me in a thick down east brogue accent. Many people in this part of the world use a dialect similar to how old English was spoken. Some refer to it as Hoi Toider (High Tider) Captain Joe often used these phrases.

One such phrase was, 'High tide, no fish, got to go home and dig taters.' All this simply meant was that fishing was not good that particular day.

Then I heard, "Got another one in the sock." That signified a fish was on the line.

Joe would tell me who the people were in the photos, what they might've done for the community, and where the picture was taken. The photographs came to life at that point. It was like watching the History Channel with a live narrator. Similar to a time warp, I could be transported to the era the picture was taken. Joe awakened all my senses. I could feel my legs churning along the unpaved roads. I could smell the odor emitting from the fish houses. I could hear fishermen yelling back and forth on the docks. I would learn a lot about Swansboro during my short visits.

Saltwater was not in my blood, but salt air slowly became intoxicating to my senses. The history of the area became intriguing. The culture became one that I would embrace.

There was also an abundance of pictures showing Joe's boats across several decades. Tons of fish could be seen in most of them. Men and women that hired Joe for charter, held up what they had caught on that particular day. Some photos were in black and white. Additionally, many of the fish were so big they were either held by a large hanging hook or simply laying across the docks. Those fish, I'm told, weighed hundreds of pounds. I'd ask Joe what types of fish they were. He answered me from the comfort of his recliner. There was a Mako shark, weighing 297 lbs. That shark was caught in a tournament. There were bullhead dolphins, also known as Mahi-Mahi. Wahoo, Sea Bass, Blue Marlin, Cobia, and many others were also displayed. The sight of the different types of fish mesmerized the inquisitive teenager that I was.

Walking around that house built in 1933 put life in perspective for me. I might as well have been in a museum with all those hanging photographs and loose artifacts spread throughout the house. Ivory figurines from Africa sat on desks and the floor. Duck decoys from the Harker's Island Decoy Festival lined up on shelves. Other antiques filled the homey living quarters. Made me feel small in a good way, knowing life was much, much bigger than myself.

During the first few months of Captain Joe and mom dating in 1994, I was asked if I wanted to go deep sea fishing on the Billy Anna II. Once I had the opportunity to go, Joe drove me to where his vessel was docked at Dudley's marina. Upon first sight, Billy Anna II resembled the boat from the television show, 'Gilligan's Island.' I vividly recall untying the ropes from the cleats that secured Joe's boat and then setting off for the Atlantic Ocean.

Passengers on passing boats waved at us, no matter if they were commercial fishermen or families out for an afternoon cruise. I waved back. The Billy Anna II appeared to be slower than the passing boats, but we were much larger than most. After making our way through the hazardous, shallow channel, we crawled at a snail's pace through Bogue Inlet. Soon as we found the deep waters of the Atlantic Ocean, Captain Joe accelerated the boat and cruised around fifteen knots.

Between the rolling swell of the waves and the speed of the Billy Anna II, I grabbed the nearest railing and held on for dear life. Up and down, up and down we went, going out further and further into the depths of the ocean. At one point I closed my eyes to soak up the moment. My body moved with the rhythm of the rolling waves. An occasional splash of saltwater found my face. Salt air found my nostrils as I inhaled deeper and deeper. The engines vibrated under my feet, giving me a numbing sensation. The rumbling roar of those same engines made it difficult to hear anything from the other four passengers on board. Now and then I glanced behind us; the land appeared smaller and smaller. After a few peeks, it disappeared altogether. We were now in the unknown, at least to my aquatic virgin eyes. The experience was as surreal as surreal could be.

When the water smoothed out, I looked up at Joe on the top deck behind the wheel. He was in his element. Unable to communicate orally, he glanced down and gave me the 'thumbs up' gesture. I returned it with my own thumbs up, proud to be out on the water with this man. So this was what it felt like to be out here in the middle of nowhere. Joe slowed the boat down a notch and yelled out about a certain rock formation some one-hundred feet below us.

Minutes later, he claimed a sunken German warship from World War II laid beneath the boat. Both could have been true. For all I knew, the lost city of Atlantis was underneath us. It all looked the same to me, with no distinction from one mile to the next. I hadn't a clue as to how we were going to get back to shore. I peered up at Joe. His smile beamed brightly on that sunburned face, giving me confidence that he knew what he was doing and that everything was going to be alright.

Duke, the first mate, who happened to also be Joe's nephew, began scrambling around the deck. Duke's mom, Paula was Joe's youngest sister with strong Webb genes. Joe barked out jargon to Duke that only a fisherman would've understood. They had their language. Whatever Joe said, Duke seemed to have understood and performed to a T. Hastily, the first mate began breaking out fishing rods and other equipment. Duke quickly baited the large hooks and began setting the outriggers and downriggers. In a matter of minutes, Duke had four fishing lines out in the water and the poles set in gunwales. Captain Joe slowed the boat considerably and we came to a crawl; the smell of diesel fumes entered my nose. It was now a waiting game. Man versus fish.

With four large fishing rods sitting erect, their lines following behind us, the Billy Anna II trolled through the warm waters of the Gulfstream. I can tell you that there is nothing like reeling in a big fish. A twenty-pounder can

*Captain Joe Webb and dog Summer*

feel like you have a monster on the other end of the line. And a hundred-pounder may have you thinking you're reeling in a small compact car. I will also admit that when that first line started whining like a tornado that day on the Billy Anna II, excitement grew on board. Duke dashed to the rod that had hooked a fish. He allowed the fish to take the line out a little further before he set it.

Then, he looked at me and waved me over. I had the honor of reeling in the fish on the other end of the line. With all the strength I could muster,

I cranked that reel clock-wise, pulling in the fish inch by inch. Time seemed to have stopped. Joe slowed the boat down and navigated left and right to get a better angle on the fish. After what I felt was an eternity, I called over to Duke to take over reeling duties. I was exhausted. Duke shook his head 'no' and instructed that the fish was mine and only mine.

Surprisingly, I found my second wind and continued reeling. I didn't want to disappoint Duke or Captain Joe. A good ten minutes later, the first sight of glittering fins and scales surfaced. Duke and Captain Joe agreed that a Cobia was on the hook. Duke grabbed a gaff, leaned overboard, and snagged the fish with the sharp instrument so it wouldn't get away. Done reeling, I stared at the fish beside the boat. Its big eyes stared back at me. In seconds, both Duke and I brought the medium-sized fish on board. And just like that, the Cobia lay bloodied on the deck. The fight was over. We were all high fives after that, standing over the fish that I had caught.

Riding on the Billy Anna II was and is one of the best life experiences I've ever had. That memory and many others such as catching big fish would never leave me, even as I write this over two decades later. I can only imagine the numerous people affected by those experiences Captain Joe offered through chartering over the years. Just a singular boat ride will be a memory they'll have for life. I'm sure he has impacted hundreds if not thousands of people.

On a personal note, a year or two after my first boat ride with Joe, I began to get into all sorts of legal trouble. I was dabbling in drugs and abused alcohol. So much so that I was drinking more than a fifth of Jim Beam every two days and periodically snorting cocaine. My life took a turn for the worse. I got arrested time after time for possession of drugs and doing dumb things, when I drank, like fighting and being a public nuisance. The local courts were bound to put me in rehab and on probation. That didn't keep me from an even uglier collapse. I kept on doing drugs and binge drinking. One judge finally had enough. In the winter of 1998, he put me in jail for six months for violating probation.

When released from jail in September of that same year, Joe allowed me to live at his house until I figured my life out. During the next few months, Joe sat with me and discussed the bad choices that had landed me in jail. He didn't talk down to me. Simply reminded me that I had hurt my mom and others by doing what I did. He also told me that I was making life more complicated than it should be. He didn't lecture me one bit. He managed it in a way that was along the lines of 'been there done that.'

Some that may know Joe could think of him being a hypocrite criticizing me, because of his own alcohol use. The big difference between him and me would be that I was getting in legal trouble, which affected relationships with those that loved me. I was also underage. Joe's been known to drink a beer or two or a case, but he's never really gotten into serious legal trouble. Part of Joe's reputation is that he is a hard-drinking waterman like most old-school charter boat captains. During his time growing up, he saw numerous men he looked up to drink heavily. It was part of the culture. He would practice the same habits as the ones he looked up to. Another difference between Joe and me was that I mixed numerous street drugs at one time with alcohol, something Joe didn't do. As Joe said, 'I complicated my life more than it should be.' Also importantly, my brain hadn't fully developed, and I was potentially doing damage.

I could hear Joe talking to me, but I wasn't ready yet to listen to him or anyone at that point. Over the next four months of living there, Captain Joe flung out lessons on life. He taught me how to not sweat the things I couldn't control. He pounded into me to treat everyone with respect and things would be smoother for me. Joe engrained in me to shake another person's hand while looking them in the eyes. Finally, he elaborated on the difference between real friends and fair-weather friends. Though I was a hard-headed twenty-year-old his words did seep in a little. Yet, I maintained a wild and spontaneous side. Wasn't quite ready to live a peaceful life just yet.

I eventually moved from Captain Joe's house in December of 1998 when the University of High Point accepted me, some three and a half hours away. I said good-bye to the Crystal Coast but didn't say good-bye to my bad habits. My old ways continued. And instead of using drugs, I sold them in mass quantities. In 2004 the federal government had enough of my actions. I was eventually arrested and charged with conspiracy to sell cocaine and ecstasy.

I spent the next eighteen years of my life in federal prison, wallowing in regret and consequences that I deserved. During my incarceration, words from Joe echoed in my head. They finally sunk in. Tired of the consequences, I slowly began turning my life around for the better. I quit using drugs and alcohol during my fourth year of imprisonment, even if both were abundant in that volatile environment. Over time, I repaired damaged relationships, most importantly with my parents. I turned my back on my old lifestyle. I'd like to think I remained unscathed and came home a better person because of men like Joe and my father. Sure, both have their flaws but overall they are good men with great qualities to look up to.

After being released from federal prison in February of 2021, one of the first stops I made was to see old Joe. I gave him the biggest of hugs. The house or Joe hadn't changed a bit. Mom and Joe had broken up years earlier, so he was an eighty-year-old bachelor. I thanked the man for the wisdom he shared all those years prior. The man's words persisted and built a new me during my darkest hours in prison. I admitted to him that I finally had a chance to internalize most of everything he had told me. Lastly, I told him that experiences like I had on the boat with him were one of the factors motivating me to get out to do it again. It was memories of the Crystal Coast and its people that gave me constant hope. I made it out on the other side of the fire intact.

I've known Captain Joe Webb for nearly thirty

years now. He's not my real father, but he does often refer to me as one of his godsons. I take pride in that even if it's not an official title. Since post-incarceration, I visit him frequently. And even though my mom and Joe broke up years ago, they maintain a special relationship. Along the way, I've met dozens of men and women that have been positively impacted by Joe. He's influenced several generations of watermen and regular folk. Nearly everyone that's lived in this area has a story about old Joe. Those stories are a mix of legendary days out at sea, unforgettable drunken circumstances, or tales about the acts of generosity he's displayed towards the good people in Swansboro.

I think it's important to embrace men and women of Joe's age. They've been alive longer than most of us and have experiences we're not familiar with. Their stories matter and will benefit those that come after them. They are indeed arms from our past, stretching to the current day. History was the singular subject I appreciated during high school and college. I'm no historian by any means. However, that doesn't stop me from wanting to document and repeat what I've learned.

History is very important. It tells us where we came from and is used as an explanation of how we arrived at a certain point. Joe has not only taught me a little about life but he's also shared snippets of Swansboro's history along the way. My goal for this book is to repeat a handful of those stories to you. I'd love the younger locals to know more about their heritage. I also want to commemorate the families that once lived here and that are no longer with us. I want you, the reader, to know what they went through to make Swansboro what it is today. I'd love for the average person living in another state to pick this book up, read it in its entirety and say, 'Swansboro, North Carolina sounds like a nice place to visit.' Or maybe, 'I would like to have a beer with Captain Joe.'

There are a few books written about Swansboro. Two of my favorites are by Jack Dudley. Jack Dudley is a lifelong resident. He's one of the most educated men I have ever met. I can't duplicate what he did with historical photos or arrive at the depths to which he reached in the past. But I do think I can convey Swansboro's history with an emotional context. Saying that, this is not your typical history or story book. It's more like a journey that I've embarked on. I'll bounce around a little, maybe making it somewhat difficult to keep up with. I'll document what I learned and talk about the people I encountered along the way. In the course of the book, I'll mention towns near Swansboro. Each community is affected by the others. I can't wait to talk more about Captain Joe Webb and his family. I can't wait to share interviews with the citizens of this coastal town, both current and former. I can't wait to become part of the heartbeat of the seaside village of Swansboro.

# CHAPTER TWO
# SWANSBORO'S INCEPTION

It's funny. The other day I called Joe from my cellphone and told him I was ready to start the book. I asked him where he would be the following morning so we could meet up. He answered, "I never know where I'll be. If you come to Swansboro, you'll find me. I'll be wherever I am."

The following morning, I made the short drive from my house in nearby Cape Carteret in search of the omnipresent yet elusive Joe. He could be having breakfast at Yana's with the other men his age. Or he could be down at the Front Street Grocery having a cold beer no matter if it was still the A.M. He might be playing golf at Star Hill Country club. Possibly, Joe was sitting at George's Cigar shop off Church, puffing on a stogie. So, I decided to try the least likely of places he'd be. His home.

I pulled into the one-story, ninety-year-old home on Main Street. Joe's white Chevrolet truck sat in the driveway, the paint peeling off in layers. You can't miss his truck. Not only is it over thirty years old, he's got a big swan as a hood ornament. A miniature-sized version of the Billy Anna II is vibrantly painted on the tailgate, advertising the boat for charter. In addition to his truck sitting in the driveway, his twenty-one-year-old black Corvette was parked on the side of the house. Maybe I got lucky and would find him here. Knocking on the door and taking a gander through the windows, there was no sign of the fisherman. He'd already set out on his adventures earlier that morning. Guess I had to seek him out. Thankfully, Swansboro is small and quaint. Now for my adventure in finding the man I wanted to write the book with.

*Captain Joe Webb's truck*

As I previously said, Joe's house sits directly beside the one he grew up in. His sister, Paula moved into their parent's house after Mrs. Kitty died in 2003. The White Oak River lay straight ahead in full view from his porch, the same view Joe's always had. However, the big difference between today's time and the period Joe grew up in is the presence of five-lane Highway 24. It was merely a dirt path until the 1950s. Nowadays, thousands of vehicles travel on Highway 24 every day. I stepped off the porch, passed my car, and then marched in the direction of where the river met the inlets to the Atlantic Ocean. With pen and pad in hand, I took the same route as Joe had taken thousands of times. I wondered if he could do it blindfolded like I thought he could.

I once read a story about Ray Charles, the famous Rhythm and Blues singer. It's said Ray rode his bike tirelessly in the streets of Greenville, Florida during his early childhood. When he was seven-years old, Ray Charles's eyesight began fading. It was suggested by doctors that Ray had developed juvenile glaucoma. As a result, he would eventually go blind. But even after he went blind, Ray continued riding his bike up and down the same roads because he knew them so well. Since Joe had lived in Swansboro his whole life, I'd bet he could walk these same streets with his eyes closed just as Ray Charles rode his bike blind in the streets, he grew up in.

To test my capabilities, I closed my own eyes while walking down Main Street for less than ten seconds. Upon opening them I found myself in the middle of the road. Walking around blind wasn't for me. Along the way to the waterfront, I passed the same houses Joe strolled by as a kid. Some houses were over two-hundred years old. You know this because of the plaques beside the homes' doors that the historical society of Swansboro had placed years prior, telling the people that passed by what year the house was built and usually by what family. I walked slowly by each one. I couldn't wait to find out more about these old homes – in due time. I knew there was a lot of history to be learned.

After arriving at The Old Brick Building, the oldest commercial structure in Onslow County, I took a left down Front Street. Front Street is the main drag in this coastal town. Thirty, forty, and fifty years prior it was nothing like it is today. Before, the buildings were full of fish houses, meat markets, pool halls, and supply stores. They have been replaced with boutiques, gift shops, antique stores, candy outlets, and restaurants. You will hardly see men walking around in fishing garb and toting fishing gear any longer. Today you will see families strolling the downtown district wearing t-shirts and flip-flops with shopping bags in their hands.

I tip-toed across the street to Yana's restaurant in search of Joe eating breakfast. A life-size Elvis Pressley model manned the entrance. While peeking inside, old friends of mine waved at me. I returned the gesture. There was no sign of Joe. I didn't know much about Swansboro yet; however, I knew a little something about the restaurant. Yana's isn't historical but the eatery is a relic of Swansboro's past that is still thriving. Evelyn Moore, also known as Yana mama opened the doors in the 1980s. In earlier years, it was a gathering place for all the local fishermen. There, they exchanged ideal fishing spots for the day, weather conditions, and the types of particular fish that were running through the area. The interior of the restaurant is themed from the 1950s. Photos of movie stars during that era line the walls. Even an old jukebox is displayed. I could envision the restaurant full of fishermen drinking their morning coffee before the sun had a chance to come up.

*Captain Joe Webb and Evelyn Moore*

Old men still sit at the back tables each morning, but most are carpenters, plumbers, and contractors, not fishermen like previous years. Yana mama is no longer with us either, passing away in 2022. Her legacy lives on through the restaurant run by her first grandson nicknamed John-John, who has worked there since he was thirteen years old. John-John is also considered one of Joe's godsons. Evelyn and Joe were known to be great friends up until the time of her death. And as a side note, Captain Joe owns the building that Yana's is in.

Continuing my pace, I made an immediate right after Front Street Grocery. Rob Dozier, the owner of Front Street Grocery has called Swansboro home for nearly thirty years. He was once a part owner of the Yacht Club, the same bar where my mother met Joe, back in the 90s. Sadly, The Yacht Club closed down in 2018, ending a significant era for the notorious bar. Rob may not have been born in Swansboro but he's as local as local comes. Many people often hang out in front of his store, kind of like how they did in previous generations. You can't come to Swansboro and not visit either Yana's or Front Street Grocery. Both are staples of the community.

I strutted down the hill towards the water's edge behind Front Street Grocery. This section is referred to as Joe's Beach and it's where the Billy Anna is docked. A group of locals recently got together and dedicated this area to Captain Joe Webb. They planted palm trees, poured a ton of sand on the ground, and placed benches for the public so they could sit down while looking out onto the water. It's not rare to find people watching sunrises or sunsets in this spot. Joe also owns this land which has a lot of historical significance. You will hear more about that later on.

As I got closer to the Billy Anna II, the vessel rocked left and right with the mercurial current. Large ropes secured the fishing boat to the cleats on the dock. Beach music could be heard blasting from the boat, the same music my mom taught me to shag dance to. BINGO! I had found the man. Joe stood half-hidden on the stern wearing a newsboy hat, green shirt and blue jeans that I swore were from the 1970s.

Joe called me over in that thick accent he speaks in, "Come on and get down here."

Before stepping onboard, I inquired, "What are you doing old man?"

As serious as Joe ever gets, he said, "What did I tell you about calling me old man? I'm not old. And I'm fixing a stubborn oil leak."

*Captain Joe Webb on the Billy Anna II*

It irritated the heck out of Joe when I called him, 'old man.' Always has and I knew it got under his skin. I climbed down to join him, shaking his grease-covered right hand. I looked around the older but durable fishing vessel. The engine hatches were wide open, exposing the two Cummins diesel engines. Out of all the tools he could be using to fix an oil leak, all I saw was a roll of duct tape. He picked up the roll of duct tape and then wrapped a long strip around pipes in the engine compartment. After Joe moaned and groaned for a minute or two he looked back at me and addressed my puzzling stare, "Duct tape can fix anything."

Wasn't too sure about that but I didn't question him any further. I'd already tested my limits for the day by calling him an old man. Joe turned the music down and then cranked the diesel engines to life. Over and over again he revved up the throttle on high until remarking in a booming voice, "Oil leak no more! That'll do her!"

He shut the motors down. Both of us then proceeded to sit in swivel chairs bolted down at the rear of the boat. Between the warmth of the sun and the tower of the boat blocking most of the wind, it felt warmer than it was. Upon having a closer inspection of Joe, he not only wore that newsboy hat, green sweatshirt, and those dang outdated blue jeans, but he also displayed gold chains around his neck, several gaudy bracelets, and an oversized captain's ring.

Before going on with his business about the book, I noticed Joe glaring out onto the Intracoastal Waterway and chain of uninhabited islands. Sitting in silence, I briefly felt sympathy for the man I had come to admire. If the world had been going according to Joe, he'd be out in the water, chartering paying customers in search of the fast migrating Blue Fin Tuna that came around during the winter.

But, the Billy Anna II didn't move too much these days. Life took sort of a cruel turn for Joe a couple of years ago. Joe had a heart attack, forcing him to not renew his charter license – after fifty years of service. Sitting there I couldn't help but think that Joe was like a soldier with no war to fight. A hunter with no game to pursue. A boxer with no opponents. Joe's ticker slowed him down in more ways than one. Thankfully, he could still take the boat out for personal use, though it wasn't the same as years prior when the Billy Anna II roamed the waters every day. After all the things Joe had done for the fishing community, he was now a bystander. That's like having your best quarterback on the sidelines of a game. Imagine doing something your whole life and it all comes to an end. I could sense the itch on Joe to head out to deep waters.

Swansboro's current historic waterfront district exists largely due to fishermen. In the 1970s, tourism wasn't anything like it is today. Sure, we had families that vacationed here because of the beach, but the number of people that did come wasn't close to the numbers we currently have. Some of the first types of tourists to frequent the coastal area were mostly men that lived less than a hundred miles or so from the coast. They came here to fish. Groups of men pooled their money together and hired charter boat captains like Joe. Working-class men could have a big day out on the water and catch enough fish for themselves and their families to last for months. They would clean the fish and store them in their freezers. It was a means of survival while getting in some recreation with co-workers or friends. A few even caught fish and resold them in their communities.

The 1980s was kind of the wild, wild west for the fishing industry. Regulations or limitations on certain species of fish had yet to be imposed. The waters off the coast here had a surplus of every fish during this time. Also keep in mind the overall regional population was much less than what it is today, meaning fewer mouths to feed. Over-fishing and regulations would change at the end of the decade, but during the 1980's you could catch and keep fish to your heart's content. That's where people like Joe came in. Places like Swansboro, Beaufort, and Wilmington had fleets of charter boats. A fleet usually consists of four to eight fishing vessels. Swansboro had boats like the Billy Anna II, the Pole Dancer, the Nancy Lee, the Wendy Lee, Megan, and the Edna. These fleet boats usually worked together even though they were owned by different people. As a result, most boats during this time thrived with an unlimited number of charters. So much so that the captains periodically had to turn down business.

And when customers sought out a boat in this era, they didn't have the internet like we have today. The charter boats lined the docks early in the morning, signs displayed, identifying the name of the boat and captain's name for those that passed by. It helped tremendously for the captains to have charisma and personality. When potential customers walked the docks, the captains spoke to them in hopes they would choose their boat. It didn't hurt for the captain to have a sense of humor, as well.

During this time in the 1980s, Captain Joe Webb was one of the most experienced watermen around. With his reputation, personality, and sense of humor, the Billy Anna II stayed booked over one-hundred and fifty times a year. Captain Joe Webb was one of the most well-known charter captains in the Carolinas. Time and time again, he would bring back customers to shore with barrels of fish. Sometimes he caught a thousand pounds of fish in a few short hours, meaning he could return to shore to day drink. Captain Joe made it a point to be on those docks every morning, talking to those that passed by, no matter how hungover he may have been. He only missed a day if he was very sick or if something very urgent had come up.

Regulations changed the fishing industry in the early 1990s. You couldn't just go out and catch whatever you wanted. There were limits and restrictions on the size of nearly every species of fish. Some fish you couldn't even catch at all any more because of those restrictions. The ones that could be kept had to weigh a certain amount or be a certain length. In time, fewer and fewer people came to fish for livelihood but rather for recreation. This changed the chartering industry. Nothing the charter captains could do about it. The government and other federal organizations laid down the law. Fishing vessels began to disappear from Swansboro's waterfront after those regulations were put in place. Joe's personality and sense of humor helped weather the decline in customers. Thankfully, many customers continued coming back for Joe and other captains that made it through the '90s and 2000s.

Now in the year 2023, the chartering industry is highly specialized. People just don't go out to catch fish to eat like they used to. They now go for sport, just as much. For example, people might go shark fishing, whereas before, sharks were considered a nuisance to hook on the line. Nowadays, families frequently catch and release sharks. Additionally, boats no longer have to go far out in the ocean to entertain clients. They can go inshore, meaning the boat only goes out a few miles, which can save the charter captains tons of time and money on fuel. And instead of going out one-hundred and fifty days a year offshore, they can do half-day trips.

Currently, it is a crowded industry. In place of the true fleet of boats of yesteryear, you now have dozens of wannabes that oversaturate the waters. Mostly gone are men like Captain Joe Webb and boats similar to the Billy Anna II. Corporations can simply purchase a large boat, hire a captain with little or no experience, then throw some fancy stickers on the vessel and call it a charter business. Gone are the days when customers found a charter for hire by visiting the docks. Now, they go online. The company with the flashiest website often wins the business.

Eco-tours are also part of the current highly specialized chartering industry. Captains can cruise the waterways with the hopes of paying customers that want to see the occasional dolphin surface out of the water. Or the captains might stop by one of the numerous islands or sandbars. There, the customers search for seashells or sharks' teeth while hearing a little bit of the history of the area from the captain.

Saying all that, Swansboro's tourist industry can largely thank fishing for originally bringing people to the area. I'm not saying the beauty of the area isn't alluring. Far from it. It is unquestionably beautiful. But it was initially fishing that brought most people to the coast. The booming eighties is a thing of the past. However, it should never be forgotten. And many of those fishermen that did thrive eventually suffered because of government regulations put in place. However, men like Joe will admit that it was mostly a good thing. Now future generations can enjoy the same fish that the past generations caught because they weren't overfished and driven to extinction.

*Captain Joe and Charter party*

As I did some more research, I found out more about fishing boats of the 1940s and 50s – the era Joe Grew up in. I couldn't omit what I found.

I didn't want to ignore their contributions. If it wasn't for them, captains like Joe would not have been so successful. Most of the fishing vessels in the '40s and '50s were called 'party boats.' During this time, those party boats could fit dozens of customers on board at a time. 'Party boats' was a term coined by the Swansboro locals. Groups of men and women lined the docks early in the morning to begin their sea adventure. There were plenty of for-hire boats during this era.

Another big difference between Joe's boom of the 1980s and the one before him is that the fishermen of the previous era didn't venture out much past eighteen miles into the ocean. Boats like the Valhalla, the Estelle, and Eva K. stayed close to shore. Whereas Captain Joe Webb and Billy Anna II ventured out well over sixty miles daily. His generation would locate fishing holes that would become popular like the Swansboro Hole and the Hutton. It took years of patience and dragging the bottom of the ocean for deep crevices along the continental shelf. It took years of using ancient sonar devices to map out hundreds of square miles of ocean. They also had to regularly monitor water temperatures when certain fish made it to the area.

Also, the party boats of the 40s and 50s mainly bottom-fished, meaning the boat would just stop dead in the water. Customers tossed their lines out and sat there until something bit their hooks. Charter boat captains like Joe in later years would perfect the art of hunting big fish by trolling fishing lines stretching out hundreds of yards behind their boats positioned sixty miles out. However, a few captains before Joe did make that possible. Local charter boat Captain Vincent Ward of the vessel Jean Ann had been Joe's idol and mentor. He tested the waters and occasionally went offshore, proving that it was possible to make day trips, traveling as far as eighty miles out. And he even caught big fish now and then like Blue Marlin, but it was seldom at best. This would lead the way for the next generation of captains like Joe Webb.

Let's not forget that technology plays a huge part. Swansboro local Captain Charlie Buckmaster Sr. had the best boat in the area that money could buy in the 1950s. The 'Douglas' would be the first boat in Swansboro to be equipped with a ranger finder, fish finder, diesel power, and ship-to-shore Radio Loran all in one. The Douglas was the most sought-after boat, at this time. However, that technology didn't come close to what boats have on them today. As a result of growing up in the days of old-school chartering and with new technology, Captain Joe Webb landed smack in the middle of the two contrasting fishing generations. He would go on honing the craft of deep sea fishing by trial and error, helping revolutionize the charter boat industry.

After a few minutes of contemplation on the stern of the Billy Anna II, I asked Joe, "Are you ready for me to start asking questions?"

With a schoolboy grin, he said, "Are you ready?"

Seagulls flew overhead. The occasional fish surfaced out of the water near us. Hundreds of vehicles traveled across the two Swansboro bridges every minute or two. I was ready to start. I began, "Lets kickoff with your boat. Why did you name her Billy Anna II? Since it is the second Billy Anna, I assume there was a first one."

Crossing his legs and then pulling his newsboy hat down Joe answered, "Anna is my sister. She's no longer alive. And Billy is my nephew. That's her son. He was only one year old when his momma died. He now lives in Florida. I named the Billy Anna after them."

That's Captain Joe for you. He's very sentimental. Take the numerous personal treasures and keepsakes at his house. They may not be valuable in terms of money, but they are dear to Joe. They mean everything to him. Postcards, pictures, and other items represent different times or eras of his life.

I remember one recent visit to Joe's house. He showed me photos of when he had gone to Africa years prior. He tagged along with his friend Martin and ended up teaching young boys and girls how to fish there. I could see the look on the youngster's faces and how they admired Joe in those photos. And Joe's face said it all too. He loved and treasured the experiences he had in Africa with those same kids, even if there was a language barrier.

He kept on, "The first Billy Anna was purchased in 1960. Kept her for seventeen years. Went through three sets of engines, so I laid her to rest in '77. Got the Billy Anna II up near Boston that same year. Paid eight grand cash for it. They shipped it down here and I put the motors and everything else on myself with the help of my old friend W.T. Casper. She's been in Swansboro ever since."

So, you've had this boat since 1977? That's the year I was born. It's forty-six years old?" I said.

*Captain Joe Webb and one of the kids he taught to fish, photo courtesy of Martin Wiechmann*

He chuckled, "Never thought of it like that."

"Original engines?" I asked.

"I wish. No, these are the third pair. These last pair have run strong," Joe said.

I winked and said, "Just with an oil leak."

"You weren't paying attention earlier, were

you? I solved that problem with duct tape." He winked back.

Didn't argue back with him. I could not imagine what the boat had been through. We've had dozens of major hurricanes here along the coast since 1977. It's a miracle in itself to make it through one, much less numerous earth-moving storms. I've been through a lot in my life, but not nearly what the Billy Anna II has withstood in the same years.

"Did it ever get damaged in a hurricane?" I asked.

"Back in 1996, I believe hurricane Bertha or Fran messed it up pretty well. Took me a while to get it back to being seaworthy." Joe said.

"Let's talk more about your boat later on. I'm sure there are tons of stories about this boat and the people that've been on it. I want to get into some personal stuff. You were born here in Swansboro in 1941. Tell me whatever history you know about your family and how they got here. If memory serves correctly, they were one of the first families in Swansboro?" I asked.

Scratching his beard in deep thought and adjusting his legs, Joe commenced in telling me about his family, "Don't know about the first ones. Certainly, one of the earlier ones. Less than four-hundred people lived here during my parent's day. Daddy's mom's side of the family was 'Moore'. The Moore's originally lived in Diamond City, now known as Shackleford banks, the islands where the wild horses now roam." Joe said.

"Same place near the lighthouse of Cape Lookout?" I asked.

Playing with the bracelets on his wrist he went on, "Yep. Diamond City experienced a bunch of hurricanes in the late 1800s. One after another, the five-hundred people that lived on the island kept on rebuilding after each one. Then, the big one came in 1899. They called it, 'San Ciriaco.' Think back to those days, they had no weather radar, no warning. It just smashed into them. It's believed to be the worst storm ever to hit the Atlantic coast. Many lives were destroyed at the end of that century and daddy's family was part of that." Joe explained.

Joe paused before going in any further, forcing me to think of what they went through over a hundred years ago. Joe added, "Instead of rebuilding after that one, the people of Diamond City moved to places like Harker's Island, Morehead City, which they called the Promised Land, Salter Path and a few like my daddy's mom's side of the family made it here to Swansboro. I'm told there wasn't a person or house left in Diamond City after 1902, just deserted shacks and graveyards." Joe said,

"I've got tons of friends from Salter Path and Down East. What were some of the other families that once lived in Diamond City?"

"Oh, you got your Gutherie's, Lewis's, Davis's, Salter's, Styron's, Wade's, Rose's, and let me think. Yeoman's. Probably some other ones too. That's just from what I remember people telling me. Now, my grandad on my dad's side came from Durham. His family were big tobacco farmers. They got here in the later part of the 1800s. He got away from farming and started building houses."

"How about Mrs. Kitty's side of the family? How did they arrive in the area?" I asked.

Careful with his words Joe replied, "Well, mom's granddaddy, he was a Confederate soldier that got injured during a battle in the Civil War. The Yankees captured him, nursed him back to life, and gave him two options. One, he could remain a prisoner of war, or option number two was to fight with them."

"What did he choose?" I asked.

"Well, I'm here so they didn't kill him. Reckon he chose to be a Yankee for the North, hard as it is for me to say," he ended with a chuckle.

"Wait a minute. In school, we learned a term for Confederates turned Yankees. Turncoats?" I stated.

More laughter from the eighty-one-year-old, "Reckon so," Joe replied.

"So, what happened to your great grandad?" I asked.

"He lived to see the end of the Civil War. With the money given to him afterward, he purchased eight hundred and eighty-eight acres of land in what is mostly now the town of Pelletier." Joe explained.

For those that don't know the area well, Pelletier is a rural community about seven miles northwest of Swansboro. It doesn't have a stoplight or a police department. Heck, I don't even think it has an official fire department. I wanted to know more.

"So, your great grandfather bought all that land. Surely, some of it was on the White Oak River. That's got to be worth some money today.

What happened to the land? Is it still in your family?" I asked.

"When he died, he divided it up among his eight children. Since then, it's been split up in bits and pieces. Keep in mind my mom had eleven brothers and sisters. Momma eventually met dad and they called Swansboro home before I was born. I didn't see an acre of that land in Pelletier." Joe said.

That was good enough for me. I thought it was cool that he knew his roots. I barely know where my grandparents grew up at. But not Joe. He could go back at least two or three generations. Now, time to delve into Swansboro a little more.

*Ducks of Swansboro*

"Joe?" I asked. "How did Swansboro get its name? I see nothing but a bunch of rough-looking ducks waddling the downtown streets. I don't even think I've ever even seen a swan for that matter." I tried to be funny, "Guess the ducks ran them out of town."

If you've had the privilege of visiting or living in Swansboro in recent years, you'll immediately know what I'm talking about concerning the ducks. They're everywhere and they rule the land and waterfront. You cannot walk around without having to stop for them. When they reproduce in the springtime, you'll see countless yellow ducklings lined up, following close behind the hens and drakes.

These are wild animals, so to speak. However, you can get within mere inches of them. They're not scared of humans one bit. It's an unspoken rule to not harm those ducks, no matter if they are a nuisance or not. Rumor has it, that if you harm one - even if it's an accident, you'd better not come back to Swansboro. It's also rumored that your photo will pop up in the local newspaper. Don't know if that's true or not. Best believe if a flock of those ducks steps out in front of my vehicle, I give them all the time in the world. I've had my picture in the newspaper for negative things. Not the best feeling in the world. So, if you do make it here to Swansboro, be good to those ducks. I would hate for you to come here on vacation and leave on probation.

Joe laughed off the remark about the ducks running off the swans. "Swansboro wasn't named after swans or ducks. Swansboro was named after a man named Samuel Swann. At one time he was Speaker of the House of Commons back in the early 1700s. If you look at the foot of the bridge, you will see a sign dedicated to him." Joe said.

He paused before going on, "About those

ducks. About twenty, thirty years ago a family from Florida moved to Swansboro. They say, one of their sons had developed a brain tumor and the parents wanted to be closer to their family here. The son had some pet ducks on their property in Florida and didn't want to be separated from them. His family allowed him to bring several of those ducks with them to Swansboro. That's how those particular ducks got here. They are not the type of ducks to migrate like other species. They call the ones here in Swansboro, 'Muscovy' ducks. Did you know the hens can have over one-hundred ducklings a year? That's why you see so damn many of them." Joe said.

"I see. Back to Samuel Swann, Is that the large statue on the other side of the bridge?" I asked.

I could see Joe digging deep into his memory, "No, Samuel only got a sign. The statue is of Onslow County's most famous captain. Captain Otway Burns." Joe said.

When traveling, I frequently check out road signs, historical markers, and other mementos of the past. I'll often take pictures and then Google the person(s) or event(s) to learn more about its history. Why is it that so many of us tend to ignore those same signs of significance in our own hometowns? At least I'm guilty of that. I've noticed the statue in Swansboro but not once had I stopped by to see who it was. I didn't have a clue that there was a historical sign dedicated to Samuel Swann on the side of the highway.

I remarked sarcastically, "Thought you were Onslow County's most famous captain?"

*Town statue of Otway Burns*

Joe answered back with light-hearted humor, "I'm the best-looking Captain of Onslow County." He stood up and looked at the other side of the five-lane bridge and added, "Captain Otway Burns. Merchant tradesman, war hero, and shipbuilder. He was born here in the 1700s and roamed these waters as a teenager and young adult. When the War of 1812 began, Otway joined the war effort against the British. He purchased a boat up North somewhere, put a bunch of guns on it, and named her the 'Snap Dragon.' Otway and his crew captured dozens of British boats and nearly three-hundred prisoners. But he's most famous for building the first steamship in North Carolina right here in the very place you are sitting. There's a lot of history right here. We had a big whoop-dee-do back in 1983, dedicating the statue to him." Joe told me.

Joe paused before going on, "You can't see the statue from here because of the highway. Next time you go over there, check him out. You will see Captain Otway pointing in this direction."

"What's the meaning of him pointing?" I asked.

"Back in the day, I had a restaurant called The Snap Dragon after the famous ship. The Snap Dragon restaurant was right here where we are now. The statue pointed directly at the restaurant. Old Otway was my free billboard," he finished the last word by chuckling at his ingenuity. He then added, "Officially, Otway points over here because the town wanted him pointing where the steamship was built. If you look in his other hand, he's holding the blueprint or plans to build it." Joe explained.

"I didn't know you had a restaurant. Thought you always fished." I stated.

"I've had all sorts of businesses here. Ran daddy's grocery store, had a meat market, owned an arcade and a dry cleaner. Fishing is just my passion. It didn't always pay the bills. Had to find ways to supplement my income." Joe said.

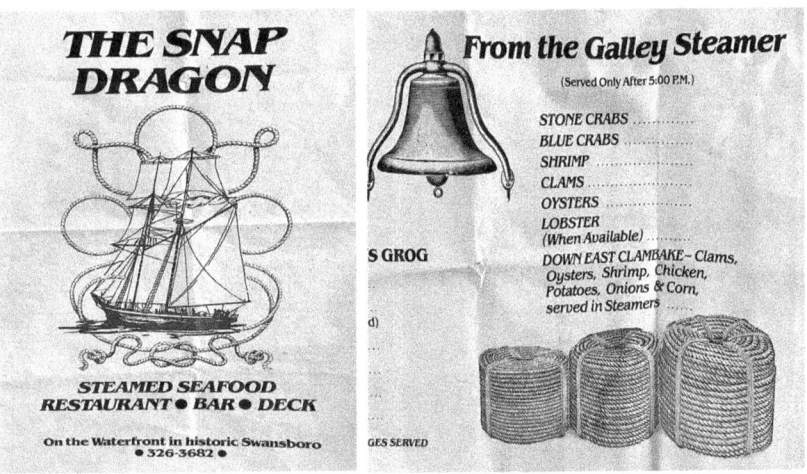

We both sat back down in comfortable silence, except for the passing of vehicles driving on Highway 24. We didn't have to talk to enjoy each other's company. Just sat there enjoying the cool breeze and winter sun. My mind was overloaded with all the information Joe had given me in such a short time. Joe had endless stories. If I asked him a question, he usually had an answer. So far, I'd only scratched the surface with all things concerning Swansboro. But I'd already learned how Joe's family made it here, facts about Billy Anna II, the history of the ducks, how Swansboro got its name, and finally, Captain Otway Burns. I couldn't wait to get back and make sense of all that Joe had told me and put it in storybook form.

The clouds moved in, making the temperature much cooler. I stood up, shook Joe's hand, and got off the Billy Anna II. However, before going home I visited the statue of Captain Otway Burns and the historical marker of Samuel Swann. Where the statute sits, you couldn't get a better view of the area. As far as the eyes can see, the barrier islands make this part of the world a beautifully painted canvas. You can also see the bluffs on the other side of the White Oak River. Captain Otway Burns stands tall for those thousands of people that regularly pass through here.

★ Captain's Table Sandwiches ★

Served with Pickles & Chips

**The Statesman** — Thinly sliced steak sandwich covered with sauteed bell peppers, onions & mushrooms, served with lettuce & tomato in pita bread

**The Snap Dragon** — Scallops, oysters & shrimp lightly breaded & fried, stuffed in pita bread with lettuce & tomato & your choice of cocktail or tartar sauce

**The Prometheus** — Lightly fried oysters, served on a sesame seed bun with lettuce, tomato & choice of cocktail or tartar sauce

**Burns Burger** — Quarter pound hamburger with bacon, cheese, grilled onion & mushrooms, lettuce & tomato on a Kaiser Roll

**Foxy Lady** — Sauteed shrimp sandwich, served with lettuce & tomato in pita bread

**The Buckstone** — Soft shell crab, with lettuce, tomato & tartar sauce on a Hogie roll

**The Zephyr** — Melted ham & swiss cheese sandwich

**Deckhand** — Hot dog with choice of sauerkraut or chili

*Mess Hall Bounty*

Oyster Cocktail

Shrimp Cocktail

Fresh Fruit (as available)

Vegetables (as available)

Clam Chowder

Instead of finding one historical marker on the other side of the highway, there were four. One was dedicated to Samuel Swann. The three signs directly beside it, represent others of Swansboro's historical importance that I'll get into later on. The statue of Captain Otway Burns and the historical signs now meant something to me. I doubted that I would ever pass the statute and historical signs again without appreciating them. I hope locals and tourists that read this will be conscious of them and appreciate them as well.

C 41

**HUGGINS' ISLAND FORT**

Confederate 6-gun fort guarding the entrance to Bogue Inlet; burned by Union troops. Aug. 19, 1862. Remains, 1 mi. SW.

C 54

**"PROMETHEUS"**

First steamboat made in N. C. Built in 1818 by Otway Burns, privateer in War of 1812. Shipyard located 350 feet S.W.

C 44

**PORT SWANNSBOROUGH**

Named for Samuel Swann. Town incorporated in 1783. Port, including area from New River to Bogue Inlet, established in 1786.

# CHAPTER THREE
## CAPTAIN OTWAY BURNS

Before moving on from chapter two, I felt comfortable enough in allowing people outside of my inner circle in on my intentions for writing this book. Even though there would be tons of research to do, personal interviews, and countless sessions of notetaking, I could envision how this book was going to look. Saying that, I've never been too scared to ask for help. In my life, I have found that people want to help. People want to contribute. People want to feel that they are part of something.

So, I posted a short message on Facebook with two of Joe's photos. Facebook friends and the good folks in the community immediately knew my intentions and seriousness about writing this book about Swansboro and Captain Joe Webb. I asked for stories about Joe or bits of history about the immediate coastal region that they felt shouldn't be forgotten.

In a matter of hours, I was flooded with over fifty texts, phone calls, and direct messages. Friends and strangers alike shared their family's history, and stories about Swansboro, recommended who I should talk to, or added their connection to Joe. People as far as Florida and New York reached out. The response was overwhelming and more than I had hoped for. I followed up on every text, phone call, and direct message. Some conversations were short. Some were long. A few turned into meetings later on. I made new friends on my quest to fill this book with stories about Swansboro and Captain Joe Webb.

In the next few weeks, I would meet people like Joe Rhue, Philip Keagy, Bobby and Norman Wells, Gloria Sanders, Charles Teachey, Diane-Redd Williams, Susan Casper, W.T. Casper, Ann Shuller, and Jim Corbett. You will learn more about them and their contributions later on. Most of their families have been here for decades if not over a century. Another unintended result over the ensuing days was people showing me private family photographs, historical documents, and other generational keepsakes that had been passed down. Strangers invited me into their homes and places of business. There, the kind people fed me invaluable information about Swansboro and the surrounding area. I was even sworn to secrecy in some of the things that I was told. Though Swansboro isn't my hometown, I began to feel a part of the heartbeat of the community, roaming from street to street. Dates, names, events, and buildings slowly became familiar to me.

It was suggested multiple times to visit the North Carolina Archives in Raleigh for more information that I was searching for. Very few books have been written about Swansboro. I doubted that I would find much there. I was on the fence about going to the Archives but with much urging from my girlfriend, I decided to give it a try. Melissa said I'd regret it if I didn't go.

Either way, I planned the trip.

That same week I filled my car up with gas and set off for the state's capitol in Raleigh. The trip would take less than three hours. Along the way I replayed conversations with Joe from my phone, recorded by another one of his godsons, Brad Nicolajsen. Brad is the son of Evelyn Moore, who was known as Yana mama. With my phone's volume on full blast, Joe's memory and experiences fascinated me. In one conversation he spoke about how he learned how to fly a plane by the seat of his pants. Mid-air, the pilot instructed Joe to take over. That plane ride wasn't so smooth, especially the landing part. Joe would go on recalling the first, last, and even nicknames of people he's known in his long life.

Less than three hours later I pulled into Raleigh. The interstate and streets were extremely busy. As I navigated my way through the downtown area, I didn't have any high expectations of finding much at the Archives. Maybe some old photographs, land deeds, and other miscellaneous stuff but not much else. I parked the car and walked towards the intended building. There was a mystery about walking into the unknown. Who knows? Maybe I would find a trove of treasure concerning the history of Swansboro, that few people knew about.

Hundreds of school kids poured out of school buses as I headed down the sidewalk. They were here for a field trip, while I was on a field trip of sorts. I passed by many of the school kids on the way to my targeted building, saying hello to them as they passed in a single file line behind their teachers. I climbed a steep set of cement steps and then marched through a set of double glass doors.

*Chad Hollamon at N.C. State Archives*

Getting into the Archives was like visiting an inmate in prison. I don't say this in a bad way. Our history should be guarded. It should be protected. First, I had to present my driver's license to a police officer at the front desk. Next, I had to fill out multiple forms that asked why I was there. After the forms were completed and cleared by the police officer, I had to walk through two corridors, then up an elevator before entering the main floor of the Archives. There, I had to fill out more forms, be given a rule sheet, and then required to wear a visitor's badge. Finally, I'm buzzed through a locked door. I found myself entering the large area of the Archives that resembled a library; it smelled like old books and newspapers. Aging paper emits this distinctive odor. I felt enveloped by history.

Bookcases, shelves, boxes, and tables filled the large area. A clerk greeted me as I walked in and offered help if I needed it. I told her that I wanted some information about Swansboro, omitting the part of me writing a book. People that write books should know what they are doing and I was clueless as could be. The helpful clerk typed something into her computer, vanished to a back room, and then came back out with at least ten accordion-type boxes on a cart.

I wheeled the cart to a nearby table and began my research. There were books, pamphlets, index cards, photographs, and newspapers inside those boxes and they all had to do with Swansboro and Onslow County. Most of what I found was given to the Archives by a local Swansboro historian named Tucker Reed Littleton. I'll talk more about him later on. He has since passed, but if it wasn't for him, most of the items in those boxes wouldn't have been there.

In less than ten minutes, I found out more about Swansboro's inception. Joe was right. The town was named after former House of Commons speaker, Samuel Swann. I did find information that Joe probably wasn't aware of. Or maybe he is. A man named Theophilus Weeks started the town that is now Swansboro on his plantation in 1770.

Before Swansboro got its name, the area was called many things like Bogue, Weeks Point, The Wharf, and New Town. Mr. Weeks laid out six streets and forty-eight lots, each 60 -feet by 200. In 1771 the first public sale of land began. The town would be incorporated in 1773. Theophilus Weeks would become known as the 'founder of Swansboro.' Delving more into the boxes, I established that Swansboro was spelled Swannsborough until 1877. The Post Office advocated for shortening the spelling. I sat there for hours, pouring over all the history in front of me.

Captain Otway Burns would be a little more interesting. The statue of Captain Otway Burns was erected in 1983, as Joe said, coinciding with the Bicentennial celebration of Swansboro. Otway Burns was born in Onslow County in 1775. His grandfather originally came from Glasgow, Scotland. Otway became a swashbuckling seaman in his early teens, loving life out on the water. In his early twenties, Otway dabbled in both boat building and merchant trading between the coasts of Maine and North Carolina.

When the War of 1812 began, Otway was urged by his friends and family to remodel his merchant vessel into a privateer warship. A privateer is a private person or ship that engages in maritime commission of war. Otway considered his boat too slow for battle. So, he traveled to New York with cash in hand, given to him by a group of investors from New Bern, North Carolina. These investors were led by Edward Pasteur, a physician and local political leader.

Captain Otway Burns purchased a 147-ton schooner named 'Zephyr' for $8,000.00. The Zephyr was nearly 90 feet long and 23 feet wide. It had a depth of nine feet and would be armed with an array of weapons. It had one pivot gun, seven-gun carriages, cutlasses, pistols, muskets, pick axes, and blunderbusses on board. Captain Otway Burns rechristened the vessel and renamed her the 'Snap Dragon.'

Captain Otway and his crew were now privateers. Even though nearly all ships carried guns during this age, the Commission empowered the holder of a privateering license to carry out forms of

hostility permissible at sea by the necessities of war. This included boarding foreign vessels and taking their crews as prizes. The proceeds of the captured ships were often divided up between the privateer's sponsors, ship owners, captains, and crew. Additionally, a percentage share usually went to the issuer of the Commission. This meant that Captain Otway Burns and his crew were legal pirates whose duty was to eliminate the British at all costs. In doing so, it would be deemed patriotic, honorable, and respectable and in the end, would be lucrative.

Before the Snap Dragon made its first voyage, someone complimented Captain Otway Burns in a newspaper, 'Burn's experience as the Commander of a Coaster admirably fitted him for the charge of a Privateer. He had the frame of Herculean strength and tireless endurance, a mind active and acute, a courage which not shrinking, a nerve that grew steadier in fiercest danger, a temper quick but never unsettling judgment, and an iron will that compelled obedience.'

During the Snap Dragon's first three voyages, she proved to be one of the fastest boats around, enabling her to escape any trap. In the West Indies, Caribbean Sea, Greenland, and Newfoundland, Captain Otway and his crew captured five brigs, three schooners, and cargoes valued between one and four million dollars – and took on nearly three-hundred prisoners. The Snap Dragon proved victorious in every battle she fought. In today's terms, she was a force to be reckoned with.

Sadly, before they underwent their fourth voyage, Captain Otway came down with rheumatism. While he remained bed ridden in Beaufort, North Carolina, his right-hand man, Lt. De Cokely was put in charge of the Snap Dragon and her crew. They would soon find out how much Otway's experience was needed. On June 29, 1814, a British warship disguised as a merchant's vessel tricked L.T. De Cokely. The Snap Dragon, caught off guard, was quickly overtaken by the fast enemy schooner. Lt. De Cokely was killed, and the surviving members of the crew were taken as prisoners. That was the end of the Snap Dragon's career. The crew that wasn't killed off by the British made their new home on a remote island, never returning to their homeland.

Captain Otway Burns became a national war hero. He also became just as famous for something else after the war. He used his proceeds to build a steamship. In 1818, Otway launched the first North Carolina steamboat from a shipyard in Swansboro.

I was surprised to find that it was built exactly where Joe owns the land and where he keeps the Billy Anna II docked. It's the same land on the waterfront where stood the Snap Dragon restaurant that Joe opened years prior. That's some history! Captain Joe and Captain Otway Burns owned the same land. And Captain Joe named his restaurant after Otway's warship.

Otway named the steamboat he built the 'Prometheus.' For seven years, Prometheus provided service to customers between Wilmington and Southport, North Carolina. The most famous passenger to ride on the Prometheus was United States President, James Monroe. I found more

THE PROMETHEUS, completed in 1818 in Swansboro by Otway Burns, was the first steam ship to be built in North Carolina. This pen-and-ink sketch was executed by Roger Kammerer, Jr. of Swansboro.

history. After it went out of service, not much is known about what happened to the steamship. Many believe it was scrapped and used for spare parts. It's maddening that history wasn't preserved regarding the Prometheus.

A few years after Captain Otway built the steamship, he served in the House of Commons where he was eventually voted out. Guess politics aren't for everyone. I even read where some of his

peers spit at him as he packed up his belongings and walked out the door. In 1834, President Andrew Jackson appointed Captain Otway Burns as the Brant Shoal's light keeper on the island of Portsmouth, North Carolina, which at the present day is called Ocracoke. There, he and his third wife lived for many years. He would ultimately die broke and destitute on October 25, 1850.

There is a town about thirty miles north of Swansboro named in honor of the captain. It's called Otway, North Carolina. There is also a town on the western side of the state named after him. It's called Burnsville. Just like Swansboro, they too have a Captain Otway Burns statue that sits atop a mountain.

*Chad Hollamon at the burial site for Captain Otway Burns in Beaufort, N.C. Photo courtesy of Melissa Anderson.*

I sat there in the Archives for hours and only went through half of the boxes. The five o'clock hour approached, representing the time the Archives closed. I wrapped up my notes, returned the boxes to the clerk, and exited the library-like room. There was no question that I would have to return as soon as I could to dig through the other boxes. On the way out of the building, I shook the police officer's hand that I had checked in with. I thanked him and promised he would see me in a few weeks.

I climbed into my car and made my way out of the busy streets and interstates of Raleigh. During the three-hour drive, I replayed some of the recordings of Joe. When I stopped, I watched a video which showed him with a beer in his hand. A group sat around him as he spoke about his life on the water. Everyone listened intently to his stories. He always demanded an audience. He just has this way of retelling things that made you feel like you are part of the plot. Couldn't help but think that history sometimes happens right in front of our faces. It's usually not until the next day that we see its significance.

# CHAPTER FOUR
# A CHANGED LANDSCAPE

**I** found Joe sitting under a new umbrella on his porch one late afternoon. Something was a bit off about Joe. That schoolboy grin was almost non-existent as he slumped down in his fold-out chair. Finding my makeshift seat on an upside-down five-gallon bucket, I sat beside him. Like I said before, Joe and I can be comfortable in silence. We don't have to use words to enjoy each other's company.

The only thing I figured Joe to be looking at was the hundreds of vehicles passing by on Highway 24 every few minutes. Or maybe he was staring at the White Oak River. Either way, I sat there with him and looked on with him, not wanting to interrupt his train of thought. Sometimes a man needs quiet. From my years in prison, I understand that more than anyone. We just sat there on the old porch without saying a word for a good fifteen minutes before Joe broke the stillness of the moment.

He blurted out, "Change."

"Change? What are you talking about?" I asked.

Captain Joe pointed to the nearby highway and explained, "See all those trucks? You can tell the economy is flourishing and the changes they are bringing with it by just sitting here. All those eighteen-wheelers, dump trucks, and military vehicles are going somewhere. Most of them are going to build on untouched land. We have all these people who are moving here. It's going to be like Myrtle Beach here one day."

"Maybe so. You and I aren't going to be around to see it if it does." I said.

"I don't know about that. I'm watching it right now. Sometimes I just sit here and watch all the commotion going on. This land has got busy and fast. I remember sitting on my parent's porch when I was knee-high to a grasshopper's ass. It would be rare to see one car pass by every thirty minutes. They say forty thousand vehicles pass by here every day now." Joe said.

At that moment I could see his point. Imagine living in one place your whole life and then witnessing drastic changes occur from your doorstep. I tried to put myself on his parent's porch in the 1940s and 1950s. The road in front of us didn't exist decades prior. It would eventually surface as a dirt path. Sometime later, the State of North Carolina came in and paved a two-lane road. Not long ago, it morphed into a bustling five-lane highway. Not only has the road in front of us changed dramatically, but the waterways and landscapes have also been transformed.

I sat there with Joe thinking about what I've learned about Swansboro's rich three-hundred-year-old history so far. I've had the opportunity to discover stories about Native Americans, early settlers, colonialism, The Revolutionary War, Civil War, Reconstruction, World War I, prohibition, racial unrest, the Great Depression, endless hurricanes, World War II, and other life-changing events. So far I had only a generalized education of Swansboro but I just knew that I would have an in-depth understanding of this area in due time.

Just the Revolutionary and the Civil Wars alone greatly affected the people that lived here. There are tons of stories of where soldiers ransacked houses and burned stores. During those times of conflict, the White Oak River was a major standoff point for either adversary. I could only presume how tense the regular folks were during the times of war on land or out in the water.

At the Archives I read about a fort built here on Huggins Island during the Civil War. In 1861, the Confederates with the help of slaves, constructed the multi-gun battery to defend Bogue Inlet. During tense fighting in New Bern, the fort on Huggins Island was nearly abandoned for a short time by the Confederates who sent their troops to help with the effort against the North. As a result of most of the Confederate troops leaving, a regiment of Yankees overtook Huggins Island, burning the barracks and invading Swansboro. Only the earthen embankment on the island remains as evidence that a fort ever existed.

Then there were the changes the new and improved military brought to the area in the 1940s. The forming of new military bases before World War II brought an influx of tens of thousands of people that came here from all over the country to serve in the military. With their arrival, houses had to be built. The construction of stores, shops, restaurants, and other establishments was created to support the new families that would call Onslow County home.

I also thought about the natural disasters changing the way of life here and even displacing families. Take Hurricane Hazel for example, also known to be one of the greatest natural disasters to hit the state. Hazel made landfall on October 15, 1954. They say when it came through, every pier and dock on Swansboro's waterfront was torn up by the angry ocean and then violently spit out onto the streets. Because of the fifteen-foot storm surge at high tide, flooding destroyed businesses and moved houses and even larger buildings.

Wind speeds of up to 150 miles-per-hour, snapped trees in half and blew away anything that wasn't secured. Rain poured down in buckets. Dozens upon dozens of fishing vessels would end up on land as well as debris washed up in the streets. The way of life would be different for Swansboro after Hurricane Hazel, with most citizens having to rebuild or locate further inland. The storm affected the whole eastern part of the state, leaving residents with the task of cleaning up every street and road. After Hurricane Hazel moved out, it left 39 people dead, 200 injuries, and over 15,000 homes and buildings destroyed. Hurricane Hazel was one of the most catastrophic storms to ever hit the United States.

I had only learned a little bit about Swansboro so far, but I was eager to find out as much as I could on this journey I had put myself on. Joc has lived a colorful life, all of it right here in downtown Swansboro. He has been alive for nearly one-third of the town's history. He's seen the good times. He's seen the bad. He reveled with the locals when those times were good and when it thrived. And he rolled up his shirt sleeves when things got bad, helping the community out any way he could.

Captain Joe broke me out of my thoughts with a startling demand, "Chad, when it comes close to my time to go, make sure they don't take me to a retirement community home or let me die in a hospital. I want to die right here where I was born." Joe said.

I tried to take the seriousness out of the conversation by saying "Joe, you are probably going to outlive me."

"Surprised I made it this long. Getting old is a funny thing. You think about life and death a whole lot more." Joe said.

Thoughts of my own mortality suddenly came to the forefront of my mind at that point. I hadn't pondered too much on death. Just too busy living, after spending nearly two decades in federal prison. In prison, it was all about survival. Now that I'm free, it was about doing things that made me happy. It was about being around the people that I missed as much as I possibly could. Maybe that's why I hung out with Joe. From years of being incarcerated, I often wondered how he was doing in life. During those years in prison, I didn't talk to him one time, nor did we exchange letters. Life has an uncanny way of bringing people back around to you. Back in the 1990's Joe taught me a little bit about life. More than twenty years later he was making me contemplate my eventual death.

I assumed Joe to be looking at the traffic and thinking about change but that was all symbolic of what was really on his mind.

"Can you do that for me, Chad? Can you make sure they don't put me in a retirement home or let me die in a damn hospital? I want to die right here where I was born," Joe repeated himself.

I felt honored that the man would give me this responsibility. I felt privileged that he thought of me like a family member. Captain Joe had seen most of the people he grew up with already die. He was one of the last ones remaining from his generation.

I responded, "I'll give you my word, Joe. I'll do what I can to make sure you don't go to a retirement community or die in a hospital."

I wanted the conversation to be less morbid. I looked at his new umbrella and commented, "I see you got a new umbrella. What made you get it?"

"Well, the umbrella found me," Joe stated.

"Found you?" I asked.

"Saw it in the trash can by Jody Floyd's. Looks good, doesn't it?" Joe said.

Only Captain Joe Webb. Only Captain Joe

would dig through the trash and find something he could use. He's always been known to be resourceful. I was eager to learn more about this intriguing man and his little hometown of Swansboro. I left that afternoon with the short conversation Joe and I had on my mind. The rest of the day the conversation echoed within my consciousness.

The Swansboro Recreation Commission
is proud to Present

# Swansboro's Annual Mullet Festival

given for your enjoyment
and the benefit of the Recreation Program of Swansboro
on Saturday ~ October 14, 1961

## PROGRAM

1:00 ~ Parade — all around the town
2:00 ~ Refreshments in the Community Building
Concert —downtown — featuring the
Force Troops Drum and Bugle Corps
Dancing by the Jacksonville Cloggers
3:00 ~ Boat and Water Show

Car Show                    Historical Tours
see all the new Models at    conducted tours to all
Elementary School grounds    points of interest

Boat Rides
around the harbor

## Mullet Dinner at the High School

from 5:00 to 7:00

Entertainment during the Dinner hour
5:00 ~ Dinner Music by the Drum and Bugle Corps
5:30 ~ Demonstration of the Art of KARATE
by Sgt Pearson and his Team
6:30 — The Town and Country Playboys
with The Jacksonville Cloggers
7:30 — Fireworks

## Dance ~ Swansboro High School

to the music of Frank Kast and his Orchestra
from 8:00 to 12:00

Get your Tickets NOW
Adults — $1.25, Children $.75 — for the entire program !
Available at local stores or write Box 211, Swansboro
Bring your Family and enjoy the day
in "The Friendly-City-by-the-Sea"

# CHAPTER FIVE
# THE MULLET FESTIVAL

One of the biggest events held in Swansboro is the much-anticipated annual Mullet Festival. It has the distinction of being one of the oldest festivals in North Carolina. It's usually held in October, coinciding with the peak of mullet season. Mullets are an iconic fish in this area. They are also called Striped or Jumping mullet. Small fish are known to jump from the surface of the water. I've been in a boat on the Intracoastal Waterway and had several mullets jump in. These fish migrate in massive schools, making them easy to catch in large numbers.

Growing up in the area, going to the Mullet Festival on that Saturday in October was mandatory. It is borderline sacrilegious not to attend. The festival kicks off with a parade in the morning. Highway 24, also known as Dr. Corbett Avenue, shuts down for hours on this occasion. Once you find a place to stand among the sea of people, you wait for the parade to begin. When it does, you will see themed floats, a Marine marching band, clowns, various school sports teams, young girls twirling batons, firetrucks, men from the local Rotary Club driving miniature cars, the mayor, and last but not least, the reigning Miss North Carolina. It's full of hand waves, music, and candy being tossed out into the crowds. No matter how old I get this never gets old.

After the parade, all kinds of festivities begin before lunchtime on the Swansboro waterfront. The downtown streets are barricaded closed and manned by smiling and amicable police officers. Tens of thousands of people spend the day shopping at local vendors and listening to live music. The sidewalks are packed elbow to elbow. Seafood of every variety can be found. Shrimp, oysters, crab, scallops, etc. For the kid at heart, you can munch on funnel cakes, candy apples, cotton candy, and countless other sweets. Though the waterfront is crowded, you will encounter the nicest and friendliest of people. All smiles and good times. I see old friends here and always make new ones. The Mullet Festival is glorious for all ages.

I can't forget to mention Captain Joe Webb. Every festival I've gone too, I would see him hanging out near Front Street Grocery or standing in the vicinity of Yana's restaurant, engaged in light-hearted conversations with people. Each year I've had the chance to attend, I'vc never failed to catch sight of him. He's been part of the Mullet Festival experience since its inception.

I never really thought of how the Mullet Festival got started. It was just a yearly tradition carried out and part of our lives. Just didn't think too much of it, similar to the statue and historical markers I had ignored. Just something we automatically did. Now that I was writing a book about Swansboro, the Mullet Festival would become a subject I wanted to know more about. This would be a topic to ask Joe about.

One morning I pulled into Captain Joe's driveway. Both vehicles were in the yard. I parked my car on Main Street, walked through the grass, and made it up on the unsteady staircase that was long overdue for repairs. Didn't know how the man or anyone else for that matter, made it up and down those stairs. It's a struggle.

At the door, I didn't even give a customary knock. Marched right on in, after seeing Joe laid back on his worn but cozy recliner. Inside, I'm as fascinated when I walk into his home as the first time I did so, nearly three decades ago. The old photographs, artifacts, and fishing memorabilia place me in a different time than the year 2023. I plopped down on the couch beside him with a pen, pad, and recorder in hand. Golf blared on his large television set. Joe loves to play golf. He plays when he can at the local golf courses.

Watching the pros play on TV has become one of his favorite pastimes.

We engaged in pleasantries before I dove into the business concerning the Mullet Festival. When a commercial came on I announced, "The book is coming along. Wish I could write all day long but my creative window is only about three hours in the morning. But I'm learning so much about Swansboro and you."

"You're doing good Chad. People around town are starting to ask me about the book." He muted the television. "Want some sausage? Got some on sale this morning at Piggly Wiggly." Joe asked.

I turned on the recorder my girlfriend had given me. "No, thanks. I wanted to talk about the Mullet Festival today," I said.

"What do you want to know about it?" Joe asked.

"The Mullet Festival was something I first experienced when I was fourteen, or fifteen years old, after I moved here. I never knew how it got started or why it's even held. Is it a celebration of the fish?" I asked.

With the remote control resting on his lap and choosing his words carefully Joe said, "Want to say it got started in the early 1950s. I remember the year fairly well. I was playing with some chemicals one day and started a fire. Burned myself pretty darn good. After Dr. Corbett fixed me up with bandages I went to school. My teacher said I looked like a mummy and said I was showing off. Called me the class clown because she didn't believe me to be burned." Joe said.

I didn't stop Joe. I asked about the Mullet

Festival, but he went on about something else entirely. He rambled on, "The year before my teacher tried to pay me ten bucks to quit school. Said I was a distraction because I couldn't sit still. Still can't." Joe told me.

"Did you take the ten dollars?" I asked.

"Lord no. I made plenty of money at school by selling loose cigarettes and candy. Plus, the school was where the girls were. Couldn't give that up." Joe said.

"That's right. Your dad owned a grocery store back then. That's where you got the cigarettes, huh?" I asked.

"Daddy would have killed me for taking the store's cigarettes. I went to a competitor's store, a place called Bartley's. Told them daddy ran out and needed some. It was a little fib. Not once did I get caught." Joe explained.

I had to get him back on track. "Do you remember going to the first Mullet Festival?" I asked.

"Yeah, all it was back then was a fish fry at the school across the street. They turned that school into condos a long time ago." Joe said.

I asked, "What was the first festival like?"

"Nothing compared to now. Back then, only a few dozen people attended. I got my plate of food and went back to work cleaning the fish. They say it was a political thing. Mayor Lisk held it for the construction workers after completing the second bridge across the White Oak River." Joe said.

Now we were getting somewhere. I inquired, "Why is it called the Mullet Festival?"

"At that time people could make a living out

of their backyards by mullet fishing. There were sixteen fisheries in the area. The government and its regulations forced most of them to close down by the 1970s. Mullets typically run through these waters between August and November. We'd catch tons of them. They're a prolific fish, large numbers of them. But you can't catch mullets with a hook. No sir. The fishermen had to wade into the breakers and surround the fish with football field size nets. Then we used tractors and trucks to haul the nets ashore. Thousands of mullets could be seen flopping on the beaches. They are delicious if you eat them around the first of August when they spawn. They got a liver and a gizzard just like a chicken. When they fatten up and start to roe, it's personally one of the better fish to eat." Joe told me.

"Was there a parade like there is now?" I asked.

"I don't recall the first festival having it. Think that was the next one. After the first festival went so well, Mayor Lisk or someone said, 'We should do this every year.' Here we are still holding them." Joe said.

Joe went on talking about events other than the Mullet Festival. I shut my recorder off and let him reminisce. The information he gave me was enough to build on. I sat there listening to him.

The two of us made small talk and watched golf for about thirty minutes before I left. I had to do some digging about the Mullet Festival.

Joe was correct about the first gala being held in the early '50s. 1953 to be exact. The town didn't have an official name for it yet. Members of the State Highway Department and construction workers were invited to a fish fry after the completion of the Swansboro Bridge that spanned across the White Oak River. It took eighteen months of hard work to finish it. Former Mayor Lisk did organize this. It went off so well, the people of Swansboro wanted to do it again. The idea of calling it the Mullet Festival was born.

The first official Mullet Festival was held in October 1954. Since this was the time of the mullets running through local waters, there was an abundance of prolific fish to serve. In addition to the fish fry, they held parades, pageants, and dances. By 1961 over 5,000 people were attending the Mullet Festival. In the year 2022, it's said that nearly 50,000 people showed up.

Joe was correct about many of the locals back then making a decent living during mullet season. It would be a great source of income. At that time, mullets were a staple food. The military happened to be growing exponentially in the area at this time. As a result, the military bought and stored tons and tons of mullets to feed their accelerating numbers. I even found out that farmers abandoned the fields when the mullets ran through the water. North Carolina, especially in these parts, was once the epicenter of mullet productions.

Through Jack Dudley's book, I read that the purportedly largest catch for mullet in Bogue Sound was made in 1947.

A whopping 57,000 pounds of mullet flopped on the shore and then was shoveled onto large trucks before being taken to the local fisheries. Further research shows that during the Civil War, the Confederates caught huge numbers of mullet and then salted them down in large barrels. They would be stored until ready to be served to the soldiers. History also suggests that the first fish houses established in the area were during the Revolutionary War to supply the Continental Line with mullet. The mullets have a longstanding history in this area.

Sadly, there aren't many fish houses here any longer. The military does not stockpile the fish like they used to. The day of the mullet being a major industry is a thing of the past. The mullet may have a rich, nutty flavor and buttery texture but they've been given a bad name and are now used mostly as bait by the local fishermen. The Mullet Festival might not have started as a celebration of the fish, but we can reflect on the past during this occasion and see how important the mullets were during certain eras of Swansboro. I hope The Mullet Festival will be around after I'm dead and gone. I will continue attending this special celebration and hope future generations will continue the long tradition of the Mullet Festival.

*Captain Joe Webb on Joe's Beach*

# CHAPTER SIX
## HISTORICAL HOMES IN SWANSBORO

One February afternoon I drove across the two Swansboro bridges, the seaside village on the left representing a relic of our past. Reminded me of a postcard as the sun bounced off the old buildings and the aging docks stretched out into the water. It almost seemed that I was driving into an earlier century. The region has grown by leaps and bounds with new money but downtown Swansboro had preserved its old-world charm, rejecting corporate America as much as it could.

I took a left on Front Street, my speed topping out at no more than five miles per hour. Even though this was the long route to Joe's house, I loved taking this way. I can observe owners of establishments cleaning their storefronts. I get to see people out for a daily stroll, many of them looking into the glass-windowed boutiques, gift shops, and antique stores.

As I always did, I turned my head to the left when coming up on Joe's Beach just in case the old fisherman was down there tending to his boat. When I did, the darndest thing occurred. The Billy Anna II was nowhere to be seen. It was missing from the docks, ropes dangling from the pilings that had secured the vessel. Captain Joe Webb was on a sea adventure that morning. My feelings were kind of hurt because I'd expressed to Joe how much I wanted to go out on the water with him. I consistently asked him to go out into the waters. Captain Joe Webb taking his boat out is a rare phenomenon. Going out to sea would have been some kind of special. I felt left out.

I kept on driving to my girlfriend's cottage on Water Street, wondering where the old captain was. I wanted to wait by the docks until he returned from his escapade but a high school friend of mine named Billy Parkin was going to stop by and I didn't want to stand him up. We planned to discuss his family's ties to Swansboro and Captain Joe Webb. After settling into the nearly one-hundred-year old home, my friend knocked on the plexiglass door. I welcomed him in, and we made ourselves comfortable in the same living room where the idea of this book was conceived.

I would soon find out that both sides of Billy's family are longtime residents of Swansboro. He is both Parkin and Merritt. Both sides have been here since at least the early 1900s. Billy, just like his ancestors is a waterman through and through. Other than his short stint in the Army, he's been here his whole life. Billy sat there telling me about how he's known Joe since he could remember. His dad, Tommy Parkin was a great friend of Joe's. Billy recalled the numerous times he's been fishing with Joe on the Billy Anna II. His love of the water is because of men like Captain Joe Webb.

He went on to tell me about a King Mackerel fishing tournament he entered in the early 2000s in Morehead City. With a little less than three hours before the end of the tournament, Billy and his first mate had no fish on board. While wondering what he could do differently, he saw the Billy Anna II in the distance. Knowing Joe was behind the helm, Billy followed him. With Billy's fishing lines out in the water, King Mackerel began to strike over and over. So much so that he couldn't reel them in fast enough. In a span of two hours, he and his first mate caught a dozen King Mackerel, bettering their chances at winning the King Mackerel tournament. Billy and his partner didn't win that day, but he did place third. He credits that to following Captain Joe. Just by following his childhood idol, Billy landed fish that he would not have caught on his own.

Billy also told me about the time Captain Joe took his family out onto the ocean to scatter the remains of his recently deceased uncle George Alfred Merritt III. The winds were super strong that particular day. When the ashes were tossed overboard, the wind gusts blew some of the ashes back on board. Though it wasn't exactly the result the family wanted, it would be another story with Captain Joe. Billy informed me that he witnessed Joe marry and bury people at sea. Since the good old days, charter boat captains can perform weddings out at sea.

Since I didn't know how legit that currently is, I decided to research that subject to find out if charter boat captains can indeed officiate wedding ceremonies. From what I found, charter boat captains can marry couples. Just as Joe did with Billy's uncle's remains, he can also scatter human ashes at sea as long as it is at least three nautical miles out. I couldn't imagine Captain Joe doing either weddings or burials at sea, but I've learned so much about him that it doesn't surprise me one bit. As the Dos Equis commercial advertised, 'The most interesting man in the world.'

Billy added stories of the captain always tending to the sick and the elderly. Since Billy could remember, Joe frequently visited nursing homes, hospitals, and hospice facilities to check on those that came before him or those that were sick. Billy recalled Joe visiting his dad, Tommy Parkin when he started showing early signs of dementia. Tommy eventually succumbed to his condition. Of course, Joe went to the funeral to pay respects to his fellow waterman and old friend.

Billy told me about how Joe tending to his uncle and his dad had become a recurring theme. Nearly everyone that I interviewed so far or talked to about Joe, mentioned how Joe has always been known to visit the sick and elderly. Sure, I got tons of legendary drunken stories, but they didn't come close to the acts of generosity and kindness Joe displayed when people were in need. I can only attribute that to Joe's growing up in a small tight-knit community like Swansboro, where you not only knew your neighbors, you knew everyone in town. In past generations, everyone seemed to come together. Nowadays, most people don't even know their neighbors.

I'm not as old as Joe but I remember attending funerals as a little kid. There were always hundreds of people present. I recall a long procession of vehicles with their headlights turned on behind a hearse. Other cars would pull over in both directions as a sign of respect for the loss of a loved one. Sometimes the procession was led and trailed by police officers.

In the past year, I've gone to several funerals, including that of my granddad. Instead of hundreds of family members and friends being present, there were only about two dozen people there at best. Sadly, it's where we are in terms of our society. Along the way, we lost that small-town feel. We get so caught up in our jobs and daily lives we often put off visiting the sick and elderly as much as we should. We miss funerals because we 'don't have time.' Not Captain Joe Webb.

It's been said that he has never missed a funeral. It's also been said he's been there for families in their time of need, no matter his relationship with them. By accounts, Joe has been to over two hundred funerals, including that of my grandmother, twenty-five years ago. He barely knew her but that didn't stop him from driving nearly two hours to attend. That's old school. That's real-world stuff.

When it came time for Billy Parkin to leave, we stood on the porch making plans to see each other soon and for him to introduce me to the Caspers, a prominent family in Swansboro. While shaking hands, a passing boat on the water caught our attention. In all its glory, the Billy Anna II cruised the waterway much slower than any boat around it. An American flag flapped about on the watchtower. Captain Joe Webb had returned from another sea adventure. Like little kids, Billy and I speed walked down Water, Church, and Front Streets, in the direction of where the Billy Anna II docked. I am sure it had to be a sight to see two middle-aged men chasing a boat down.

We made it there about the same time as Joe pulled his boat between two pilings. Both Billy and I assisted in tying the large fishing vessel up. Once secured, we greeted the sea captain and the passenger he had on board. The passenger was a stranger to us. The black man introduced himself as Bobby. Bobby grinned ear to ear. I knew the feeling. Going out on the water with Captain Joe is a lifetime experience.

*Captain Joe Webb and Bobby with their prize*

Bobby held up a five-gallon bucket full of Sea Bass and remarked excitedly, "I was fishing off the docks this morning. Captain Joe was working on his boat right beside me. He looked over and asked, 'Want to do some real fishing?' Next thing you know, I'm out in the middle of the ocean. I caught a bunch of Sea Bass, an octopus, and a Mola-Mola, which Joe called a Sunfish. It was so big we couldn't get it on board. It had to weigh three-hundred pounds. I got pictures of it though."

That's Joe for you. Asking a stranger to go out on the water. That's always been his personality. Joe knew no strangers. That's why so many people adore him. Growing up in the area, I've heard all kinds of stories about Joe's passion for teaching people about fishing and life on the water. That smile never left Bobby's face. Joe didn't stop Bobby's experience there, once they got off the boat, Captain Joe showed him how to clean the fish at a small standup table. Using a sharp knife, he told us details about each fish and the best way to clean it. Bobby had gratitude written all over him.

I said to the stranger, "You will never forget today. Might seem like a regular day right now, but I guarantee that you will repeat this story for the rest of your life."

It was great seeing Joe in his element, cleaning fish and telling stories. Bobby, Billy, and I stood there listening to the man we admired. The water was his happy place. He simply wanted to share his love and joy with others. If people are truly born to do something, Captain Joe is the epitome of being a fisherman. After a good hour, Billy and I started saying our goodbyes. While Joe cleaned the fish, I asked if we could get together later on. He agreed to meet at his house after he had time to take a shower and grab a bite to eat. Billy and I left the two of them on the dock.

*Captain Joe Webb cleaning his catch of the day*

Hours later I sat in a golf cart in front of Joe's house. He came out with a beer can in one hand, ready for another adventure. After taking a long swig of beer, he asked, "Where are we going?"

"Just want to drive around. I'd like to know more about some of these old houses and buildings. Maybe you can give me a little history about them." I said.

"I'll tell you what I know, like I always do. Let me grab another beer first," he stated, and then went back inside.

As I waited for his return, I noticed that his house was missing the historical sign beside his front door. After all, his house was just as old as many in Swansboro that did display such a sign. That was odd. Having a closer look, the house he grew up in directly beside it didn't have one either. Joe eventually came out with two beers, one in each hand. He deposited them in the cup holders in the golf cart and then climbed into the passenger seat.

I inquired, "Joe, why doesn't your house or the one you grew up in have a historical sign beside the door? Your house is as old as many that do. Doesn't it have historical significance?"

Between sips of beer, he admitted, "We grew up on the wrong side of town. Us poor folks on this side of Swansboro didn't get one."

"But they have a historical sign on the house two doors down from you."

Joe gazed in the direction I was talking about and said, "That's where it starts. Are we going to ride or just sit here?"

I pressed the accelerator and proceeded with my tour. I stopped a few houses down in front of what appeared to be the biggest house in all of Swansboro. Joe looked at it while drinking his beer.

"What's the story with this house?" I asked.

"A good friend of mine, Billy Underseth's family used to own this house. They call it the 'Green House.' On the record, it is the oldest house in Swansboro. Some say it's the oldest house in all of Onslow County, built-in 1770. See the wall around part of the property?" Joe said.

*Historical Marker*

*Jonathan Green, Jr. House*

"Yes sir," I said.

"Those are ballast stones used on ships to counter their weight when they went back out to sea. At one time the town was full of them. I remember when I was younger, the whole waterfront had tons of them laying around. When sailing vessels or schooners came in, they unloaded the ballast stones and then filled their ships up with local products like tar and turpentine. Billy Underseth used some of the old ballast off my property for this wall here. Billy is in a nursing home behind Hardees now. I visit him every other week. You should come there with me sometime to meet him." Joe said.

"I'd like that. Who lives here now?" I asked.

"A guy named John McDaniels. Don't know too much about him. He's doing a helluva job remodeling it to its old form though." Joe said.

I remember reading about the Green House

when I was at the Archives in Raleigh. It's called the Green House because Jonathan Green Jr. built it. His dad, Jonathan Green Sr. was the first man known to settle his family here. When Green Sr. died, Theophilus Weeks, the man who would be responsible for plotting the streets and lots in Swansboro, married Green's widow named Grace. Grace would move in with Theophilus on the west side of Main Street in a house that had been built by Jonathan Green Sr. They lived there for a few years before he moved her to his plantation. So we got the first man to call this area home in Jonathan Green Sr. and you got the 'Founder of Swansboro,' both marrying the same woman. Astonishingly both of them were from the same town in Massachusetts. Green's son remained in this house until he sold it.

We sat there looking at a piece of history. The house was over two-hundred and fifty years old. I could only imagine the number of families that once called it home. The house had been through several wars and countless hurricanes, yet, it remained intact, close to its original form.

"Move up a little to the next house," Joe demanded.

I obeyed and stopped at the very next house across the street. I asked, "What about this one? What's the story on this house?"

"They call this the Ringware House. Built by Captain Peter Ringware around 1780. They almost tore it down back in the 1970s. It was looking bad. Thanks to Tucker Littleton, the house was cleaned up and updated, eventually being sold into the hands of a family that has maintained it since. Kids used to play in it when it was nearly abandoned years ago. Tucker got those same kids that played in it to help clean it out. It took years to get it looking like this. It's one of the only houses around to have a cellar. Most people don't have cellars in Swansboro because of the flooding. The cellar in this house is huge." Joe told me.

After a minute or two of silence, Joe instructed me, "Keep going till you get to Water Street."

A block later the golf cart stopped in front of a building that resembled an old church without a steeple. Joe went on, "See that building on the left?"

"Yes. Looks like an old church. It's called Jess's Boutique. I know the owner of the store. Jessica."

*Baptist Church*

"It is an old church. A Baptist church. Growing up, the preacher put speakers outside on Sunday mornings. During the service, half of the town could hear the sermon from their front porch. Those speakers were loud. I reckon the preacher wanted everyone to hear what he had to say. Built-in 1897, it was the first sanctuary for the Baptists in Swansboro. It hasn't been used for a church in over fifty years." Joe said.

I glanced around us and asked, "What about behind us? That's an odd brick building for Swansboro." I inquired.

Joe craned his neck back and commented, "Don't know why or how but a power company bought the property about thirty years ago and demolished the old building that stood there as long as I could remember. The power company promised the façade would match Swansboro's charm, but I don't see it one bit. Pissed off a lot of locals at the time. Before they tore it down, the building that stood there had the Rigg's Store in it. Also, Dr. Corbett's office was there. You'd always see people standing outside of it, waiting for the doc to see them. Upstairs was the Masonic Lodge." Joe said.

"History erased. That's sad." I commented.

"Yep," Joe answered casually.

He looked over to the other side of the street and said, "That's the Bartley House right there. Remember me talking about the Bartley Store, my daddy's competition? That is the same family. Probably the oddest house downtown. Its kitchen is separated from the rest of the house. Some call it a shotgun kitchen, built so smoke or aroma from the food cooking would not spread through the rest of the house. Daddy told me it was once the local post office. Also told me it was a milk house because of the gilded-aged vents. I'm not sure what a milk house is. Daddy said a lot of things I didn't understand. Before the Bartley House, it was the first hotel in Swansboro."

He continued, "Back to the other side of Water Street. Two houses behind the old Baptist church is known as the Beaufort House. See it?"

*Beaufort House in the forefront*

I nodded my head yes. "Why do they call it the Beaufort house?" I asked.

"That house is about two-hundred years old. Local tradition says it was moved here by barge from Beaufort, North Carolina by Captain Thomas Thomas. Phillip Keagy's family has owned it since the 1950s. Phillip is an old friend of mine and he used to be one of my first mates. I've known him for a long time." Joe explained.

I took a left down Water Street and parked in front of the Beaufort House. I got out and took a few photos of the house moved by the barge. Joe stayed in the golf cart, sipping his beer. I had recently met Phillip Keagy, a super nice guy.

Like most long-time residents here in Swansboro, both sides of his family were from here. His dad was Walt Keagy. Back in the 1950s, Walt owned a soda shop on Front Street that was popular with the kids. It's said he had an assortment of flavored drinks and various types of candy that kids couldn't get enough of. Most of all, Walt always had a television set on. Since TV's were a rarity in the '50s, many people came to Walt's Soda Shop just to watch TV, as they sipped on their favorite drinks. And Phillip's mom was a Barfield, a common last name during this era. Phillip recently moved back to Swansboro after years of living in Wilmington, North Carolina. He currently works at Dudley's Marina.

I made a right down Moore Street. Less than a block later, we found ourselves on Front Street. Making a right turn, hundreds of people walked in and out of restaurants, antique stores, gift shops, and other establishments. Nearly everyone we passed waved at Joe in the passenger seat or said something to him. Young children, middle-aged men, and even old ladies acknowledged the man that was my passenger. It felt like we were in our own Mullet Festival parade. Joe returned their waves, commented back to them, or asked how they or their loved ones were doing. Joe was not only familiar with that certain person, he knew their families, their children, or their significant other. Hell, he even knew many of their pet's names. I didn't have an inkling as to how Joe kept up with it all, but I admired the man's old-school mentality.

*The Brick Store*

Smack dab in the middle of town on Front Street, we passed one of the most identifiable structures in the downtown area. It is an old brick  building, it is officially called The Old Brick Store. From what I learned at the Archives, the land itself was once owned by no other than Captain Otway Burns. A wealthy merchant, named William P. Ferrand purchased the property from Otway around 1805 for $400.00. Ferrand was the town's postmaster from 1817-1836. The original store he built on the property was constructed of wood and opened in 1819. When a massive fire in 1838 burned half of downtown Swansboro, Ferrand's store would fall victim to the inferno. The following year it was rebuilt out of brick shipped from England. The foundation was made of the same type of ballast used at the Green House. It's noted that when Ferrand had a turpentine business, over 5,000 barrels lined up on Main Street weekly. William P. Ferrand died in 1847.

If you look at the top of the building, you will see a circular window with a star motif. It's said a light once beamed brightly from a lamp there and was used as a navigational beacon for boat pilots during the days of schooners and sailboats. Over the last two hundred years, the brick building has been used by several organizations and served as a merchant store, post office, church, auction house, dentist office, warehouse, and drugstore. In the year 2023, it is Lovely's Boutique, a clothing store for women. How times have changed but the oldest commercial structure in Onslow County maintains the same look as it did from two-hundred years ago.

Over the next hour Joe and I cruised Church, Elm, Walnut, Water, and Broad Streets. We stopped in front of dozens of houses with historical signs beside their doors. Some notable homes we came across on Water Street were that of Edward Hill, James Parkin, Thomas Merritt, Bloodgood, and Littleton houses.

On Elm Street, I heard about the Hawkins, Carl Sanders, Clyde Pitman, Holloway, and more Littleton and Bloodgood homes. There's also a house that was once used as a Methodist Parsonage. A Methodist Church was located beside it on the corner of Elm and Church Street but has since been torn down. We also stopped in front of Joe's grandad's house on the same street. Charles Webb built the uniquely shaped house in 1898. At the time it was built, Charles's family was growing so fast that he had to build another house that was two stories high on Church Street. Charles and his brother Ernest were both carpenters and would go on to build several houses in Swansboro. Charles lived in Swansboro until his death, while Ernest made a life for himself in Morehead City. Both men have their names displayed on historical homes in the downtown area. Today, numerous Webb descendants live within five blocks, including Captain Joe Webb, his cousin Horace and his sister named Paula.

Some of these houses in Swansboro predate the Civil War. Altogether there are over fifty historical homes in downtown Swansboro and a multitude of businesses. The town has done a magnificent job in preserving the Old-World look. If someone comes in and purchases a home, they can't just come in and modify it to their heart's desire. They can't come in, tear it down and build something new. All things must go through the town. For the sake of history, I believe this to be a good thing. With these safeguards, Swansboro will maintain this charming look for a long, long time.

Pretty soon, Joe complained that he had to use the bathroom. Guess those beers ran through him. I dropped him off at his house, shook his hand like I always did, and promised to see him the following day. I couldn't wait to get back to read the notes and study the pictures I had taken while on the golf cart. I could write a chapter on each of those historical homes but it would make this book a thousand pages long. In the duration of this book, I hope to at least mention the family names to honor them. My apologies in advance to the families that I didn't dive deeper into. They are just as important as the next.

About the time I wrapped this chapter up, I got a call from an old friend named Melissa Webb. I had gone to West Carteret high school with Melissa and her sister Lindsay. Melissa saw my Facebook post about Joe Webb, called me, and said she thought she and the captain were cousins. Before her grandmother died, she left Melissa and Lindsay with a box of papers and family photographs.

I asked why she thought she and Joe were cousins other than the last name. Melissa admitted that her great grandad was Ernest Webb, Joe's grandad's brother. WOW! I immediately requested that we meet. Before we did, I confronted Joe about his great-uncle in Ernest Webb. He had no recollection of the man. Ernest wasn't living in Swansboro around the time Joe was growing up. I couldn't connect the dots yet but knew it would only be a matter of time.

Melissa Webb, Lindsay Webb, and I met up one afternoon in downtown Swansboro. They brought the box of papers and family photos with them that their grandmother had left before she passed. We quickly concluded that their grandad Milton Webb was Ernest Webb's son. With that information, we figured that Milton and Captain Joe Webb were cousins. Joe and Milton never met because Ernest had moved to Morehead

*Charles Webb*

City before Joe was born. The reason he relocated his immediate family was that he took a job as a bridge tender in the eastern part of Carteret County. This was an era before the Swansboro bridges were built. The trip from Morehead to Swansboro would have been a three or four-hour boat ride. Families didn't travel then like we do now.

Milton, Ernest's son was born in Harlowe, North Carolina, and made his life in Morehead City. He would go on to marry Melissa and Lindsay's grandmother. There isn't much of a trace that he ever came to Swansboro. He wouldn't have known many of his relatives, including his cousin Joe Webb. The same day that Melissa and Lindsay came to Swansboro, I introduced them to their cousin, Captain Joe Webb. The four of us sat on the back of the Billy Anna II for about an hour as they caught up on different relatives. As I sat there in near silence, I could see the happiness in the sisters' faces. They had found a long-lost relative. This book thing was bigger than me. It was connecting a family that never knew each other existed. It allowed me to dig deep into history and for me to share it with you. I could have stopped the book here and been content with the results.

Sometime later I introduced Melissa to Joe's sister Paula. We met at the same house that Joe grew up in. Included is a photo of the first reunion. You can instantly see the similarities between Paula and Melissa even though they have a thirty-year age difference. Inside the house, Melissa showed Paula an endless number of family pictures. I just sat there, happy to be part of this beautiful moment. I could see the joy emanating from the two women that looked alike. By far one of the best experiences that I've been part of. The Webb family of Swansboro was going nowhere anytime soon. I could only envision the satisfaction Melissa's grandmother was having in heaven, seeing her granddaughter meet relatives because of the family pictures she left behind.

More satisfaction came that day. In one such photo that Melissa had, a young man with protruding ears stood tall and straight. On the

back, it read, 'Uncle Charlie Webb.' I got goosebumps and Paula shed a tear. She had never seen the photograph of her grandad. I just knew that the same picture would have to be shared in this book.

*Melissa Webb and Paula Webb*

*Chad Hollamon and Joe Rhue*

# CHAPTER SEVEN
## MR. RHUE AND THE HISTORICAL SOCIETY

**I** pulled up in front of Joe's house the following day. Joe was out in the yard holding a roller paint brush, all the while, white paint dripped on the ground below his feet. I figured him to be painting his house but instead, he painted the driver's side of his truck. I stepped out of my car and approached Joe.

"What are you doing?" I asked incredulously.

While rolling the paintbrush side to side on the truck he answered, "What does it look like, genius? I'm painting. The truck needed it."

"You can't paint your truck with that paint. It's not the type used on automobiles." I told him.

"Well, why not? Is Lowes or Home Depot police going to arrest me? There are no rules on this. It looks pretty good doesn't it?" Joe stated.

At that moment I did notice that it looked pretty darn good. No longer was paint peeling off in layers. Sure, that might change with our first big rainfall but it didn't look bad at all. It looked great, minus the paint dripping on his grass. Didn't appear to be the same truck as before. I also noticed the paint on Joe's clothes. He had made a mess.

Joe had more surprises in store for me. He

added, "You should see the rest of the house. I painted my deck, the stairs, and my refrigerator. Go check it out."

Joe proved to be no Picasso. Swaths of white paint could be seen on the grass leading to the deck. Inside the house, Joe had scattered paint throughout the house, including on his couch. I darted for the kitchen. He didn't lie. The refrigerator had a fresh coat of paint on it. Joe had gone crazy with the roller brush. He stood behind me with that signature grin, proud of his work. I should have taken the roller brush away but let him play the part. Spots of white paint even covered his Newsboy hat. It was like a kid had gotten into the paint.

"Want a roast beef sandwich? Got some meat from Piggly Wiggly this morning," he asked.

I took Joe up on his offer this time. I made myself a roast beef sandwich with mayonnaise and fresh tomatoes in the kitchen that resembled more of a galley on a boat. While eating on the couch in the living room and with Joe sprawled back in his recliner, I asked, "Someone told me yesterday you saved a bunch of people's lives off the coast here. Is that true?'

With his feet elevated he answered, "Wouldn't say a bunch. Sometimes the Coast Guard couldn't get out in the water in time. Many of the captains responded to emergency calls put out on the radio in previous years. Happened all the time."

"I'd love to talk about one particular time. People want to hear these kinds of things. I heard a boat sunk offshore here in the late 80s and you happened to be the first person to arrive. They say you saved four lives that day. Does that sound familiar?" I asked.

"You must be talking about Stu's boat. Yeah, his boat sank about fifteen miles out. I want to say that was 1988. Not quite sure. But I do remember it being cold as ever. I'd say late November or thereabout. I was chartering at a place we called the Honey Hole that day. A May Day went out on the radio on channel seventy-one. A friend of mine that ran the Dolphin I, Tommy, put out an alert about a boat sinking a few miles from where we were fishing. Said that I knew the boat that called for help. We seemed to be about ten miles out, so naturally, it was my responsibility to get there. I knew they were around the 27 and 39 lines. Thankfully, there were already three or four boats looking for them.' Joe said.

'We didn't even reel the fishing lines in. I just gunned her as fast as she would go after getting the call. On the way to the coordinates given to me, I kept in mind how strong the current was. While calculating where they could be, the people on board the Billy Anna threw everything on deck in no order at all, fishing gear strewed every which way. Figured with the speed of the current, they were about five miles from where they called from. While moving fast as a racehorse at the Kentucky

Derby, we started coming across floating fishing poles, lifejackets, and other debris, so I knew we were close.' Joe said.

'Minutes later, two people holding onto a cooler in the water waved me down. They were not wearing life jackets. The Billy Anna pulled up beside them. I recognized one of them as my buddy's dad. We got his lady friend on board first. She violently shook even when we wrapped her in blankets. It took the strength of everyone on board to lift Stu's dad. When we did, I asked him, 'Where's Stu?' Stu's dad was out of it and couldn't tell me where his son was. Not sure he would have made it in the water another minute.' Joe explained.

'After Stu's dad and his girlfriend named Betty were okay, I continued following the debris in search of Stu and another man they had on board. I spotted them about three miles later. They weren't wearing life jackets either. I pulled up to the nearest man near me. We yanked him on the Billy Anna. The first thing I noticed about him was he wore no clothes. He had to take those heavy fishing bibs off so he could swim. He too was covered up with anything dry we could find.' Joe said.

'Minutes later, we got right beside my buddy Stu. He was in bad shape. Not sure he would've made it another minute either. Now Stu was a big guy. 220 or 230 pounds. Took some muscle to get him on. When we finally did, he lay on the scattered fishing equipment, looked up, and saw me. I remember the words he said to this day. He said, 'Joe Webb, you are the prettiest thing I ever did see.'" Joe said.

I interjected the rescue story, "You saved their lives. I'd think you were the prettiest thing too. Did you get a medal or something for saving their lives?" I asked.

"Oh, we wouldn't be out of the woods yet. No sir. Keep in mind it was fifty-some degrees that day. Hypothermia can set in. I radioed Dudley's Marina and said I located the people on board whose boat had sunk and was coming in and needed medical attention. I put the Billy Anna at full steam at around 23 knots. Figured it take a good thirty, forty minutes to get there. Along the way, the Coast Guard radioed me and told me to stop. They wanted the passengers on board with them. With one look at Stu's dad and his girlfriend, I knew they weren't going to make it if I waited for the Coast Guard. They called me over and over again ordering me to stop. I could see their emergency lights behind me, but I wasn't stopping. Finally, I got back on the radio and said, 'You're breaking up,' and slammed the damn receiver down." Joe said.

"What happened next?" I asked excitedly.

"Bout thirty minutes later we approached Dudley's Marina. There were firetrucks, ambulances, and over a hundred people waiting on us. Fast as I could, I pulled Billy Anna to the docks. The boat was swarmed with rescue personnel. Stu's dad, his girlfriend, and Johhny, Stu's right-hand man was taken to the hospital." Joe told me.

"So, you saved the day," I said.

"Part of life on the water. Some bad things

can happen out there if you are not careful. That ocean can swallow you up and spit you out. Stu and his wife Angie Keel have been friends of mine for decades. They live in Florida now, yet we keep in touch. Stu owned a carpet business back in the day. He tried to give me free carpet for life but I couldn't take it." Joe said.

I finished my sandwich and asked, "Do you have some more stories like this?"

Joe sat there in silence for a second or two then answered, "Tell you what. I want you to meet a guy named Joe Rhue. He's got some stories and he knows just as many people in Swansboro as I do. Joe owns the antique store on Front Street called Poor Man's Hole. He is there every day. Go check him out."

"I've heard his name a few times. I'll stop by there after I leave here. Another thing. Mom says you got a DUI around that same time you saved Stu and Angie. Did you ever get in trouble for drinking and driving?" I asked.

"Two times but I never got a conviction. I'm not proud of it either. That one time your mom was talking about, the Emerald Isle police pulled me over and forced me to walk a straight line with one shoe on. I had lost the other shoe while shag dancing earlier that night at Rootie's nightclub. When they made me walk, I asked them, 'Who can walk straight with one shoe?' Anyhow, since they made me perform the test with one shoe and gave me a DUI, the judge ended up throwing the case out months later." Joe said.

Only Joe. I changed course, "I'm sure you are well aware of the legend behind another drinking incident a long time ago. A lot of people talk about it. Might be true, or might not but rumor has it, you were at the Swansboro Rotary Club one night. They were having a special dinner for a group of Japanese Rotarians who were visiting the area. During the dinner, someone's wife asked the Japanese guys how their day had been. A few of them with thick Japanese accents simultaneously answered, 'F**king great.' Confused, the wife asked them another question, 'Are you enjoying your stay here?' Again, they answered, 'F**king great.' The wife was astonished by their language. She asked where they learned to say such things. They all pointed at you at the bar and said, 'Captain Joe Webb.' You took them fishing earlier that day and taught them how to cuss." I told him.

Joe stared at me sternly while picking at his teeth with his fingers and said, "Maybe something like that happened. I'm getting too old to remember."

"Ha! So, you are old?" I asked with a hint of sarcasm.

I continued with the story, "Word is that you drank a few beers at the bar that night. Then later on they say you were in the parking lot drinking Fireball whiskey from a bottle. Your friends tried to grab your keys to your Corvette to keep you from driving but you were persistent about getting yourself home. You told them in a slurred speech, 'I got it, I got it. Don't you worry about Captain Joe Webb.'"

Joe started smiling. His ears perked up. He knew where I was going with the story. He asked,

"Where did you hear this story? I will tell you this. In my defense, the bottle was nearly empty when I got it."

"I have sworn not to tell you who told me. Let's just say it was a good friend of yours at the time. Anyhow, the legend has it that you got behind the wheel and drove home that night. Almost there, a Swansboro police officer pulled you over right in front of your house. He came up to your car and said, 'Mr. Webb, do you know why I pulled you over?' You answered, 'No sir.' The police officer responded, 'I pulled you over because you were only going eight miles-per-hour in a thirty-five miles-per-hour zone.'"

Joe butted in and said, "At least I wasn't speeding."

"No, but then you told him, 'Well, what do you expect, officer? I'm f**ked up.'" I said with a laugh.

At the last word, both Joe and I simultaneously busted out laughing – til we cried. We continued in tears for a few minutes. I've heard all kinds of stories about Joe's drinking. Most of them have been when he was out on the water. I'll share more of those in later chapters. The person that told me the story about the night at the Rotary Club also informed me that Joe was brought into the police station to take a breathalyzer test that night. The results came up to be less than the legal limit. What happened was Joe's doctors had prescribed him medication earlier that week and those pills were not supposed to be mixed with alcohol. Joe didn't read the instructions or the side effects of the medication. He's lucky he didn't hurt himself or anyone else.

I left Joe's house later that day and made my way to Front Street. I parked behind a classic 1948 Chevy Sedan. The license plate read, 'Poor Man.' I entered the antique store called The Poor Man's Hole. Inside, there was every item a person could think of in terms of antiquities. Old watches, books, pictures, figurines, trinkets, chairs, desks, and many other artifacts lined the endless shelves and hung from the ceiling. A man with silver hair sat at the back of the store behind a makeshift desk. I concluded he was Joe Rhue, the man Captain Joe had told me to come to talk to. We introduced ourselves and I proceeded to tell him about the book I was working on with Captain Joe Webb. Mr. Rhue and I instantly hit it off.

For hours we spoke at length about Joe Webb and the people of Swansboro. We bonded so well that he eventually brought out a box of old photos and newspaper clippings he had kept over several decades. It was like a mini-Archives find with lots of goodies I could use for the book. I made a new friend in Joe Rhue. He answered each question the best he could. He didn't remember details like Joe Webb, but he was well aware of events that I asked him about.

During my first encounter that day with Joe Rhue, the following is what I learned about him and his family. Mr. Rhue was the youngest of five kids. The first known Rhue in the area was Mr. Rhue's grandad. Thomas Rhue was an elder of the Primitive Baptist Church near the town of Pellitier from the mid to late 1800s. The church his grandad attended remains a standing structure today.

Primitive Baptist Churches are a rare breed, found primarily in the Southern States. Ministers of the church require no special training because Primitive Baptists believe God can call on anyone to be a minister. 'Primitive' means original or the first of its kind. They are also known as Hard Shell Baptist, Foot Washing Baptist, or Old School Baptist. One of their practices that is most different from other denominations is that of washing feet during ceremonies. The practice involves bathing the feet of a fellow church member which is usually followed by words of support and fellowship.

The building where The Poor Man's Hole is located has been in the Rhue family for nearly eighty years. Back in 1946, Mr. Rhue's dad, Jabez also known as 'Jaby' and his uncle Joseph bought the building from J.T. Bartley. In 1949, Jaby bought out his brother's share of what was then Rhue's Hardware store. From 1947 to about 1968, he operated the hardware store under that name. Mr. Rhue's mom had a beauty salon upstairs from the hardware store up until Jaby began having health issues.

Both Mr. Rhue's mom and dad decided to call it quits from their businesses. After the hardware store and beauty salon closed, the building would be used for various other businesses until Joe Rhue, the man that sat in front of me, moved back to Swansboro from New Bern, North Carolina. Since June 2012, it's been called Poor Man's Hole antique store. The original Poor Man's Hole was located on Water Street where countless boats were built from the 1930s through the 1960s. Mr. Rhue and his lovely wife have lived above the antique store for nearly two decades and the Rhues have retained ownership of the building for close to eighty years.

Being seven or eight years younger than Joe Webb, I could tell Mr. Rhue looked up to the captain in many ways. He told me stories about Joe Webb from growing up in Swansboro. Many were funny but some were heartfelt. One Christmas, Captain Joe Webb dressed up as Santa Claus for the kids in town. He put on a red Santa outfit and played the part quite well, I'm told. And there was the time Joe Webb owned a grocery store on Front Street. Joe would give anyone credit. He never let anyone go hungry. Even if a stranger was hungry, Joe

Webb fed them. Additionally, before Uber Eats, Grub Hub, and all that, Captain Joe delivered food and groceries to everyone in Swansboro that needed the service.

I was told of the time a family was in town and in dire need to get back to their hometown in Georgia. The problem was, they had no money. Captain Joe gave them money and supplied them with enough food for them to make the return trip. Mr. Rhue showed me a letter the man in need wrote years later, thanking both Joe Webb and Joe Rhue. That's Joe Webb for you with his old-school mentality. And I was beginning to think the captain rubbed off on Mr. Rhue too with his kindness and generosity.

Two important things occurred during this first encounter with Mr. Rhue. For one, Mr. Rhue allowed me to take the box full of photographs and newspaper clippings home with me. I took that box home and poured through the contents. There would be a lot of information to go on that would assist me on this journey. Additionally, many of the photos in the box would be of Captain Joe Webb and used for the contents of this book. You will see a handful of them as we move along, including the time Joe dressed as Santa Claus. Secondly, Mr. Rhue promised to introduce me to members of the Historical Society of Swansboro the following week. Mr. Rhue would help me with things Captain Joe Webb might not have had. But more importantly, as I said, I made a new friend in this man. One of the most cordial human beings I had ever met.

True to his word, the following Thursday I was

brought to the meeting place for the Historical Society. Meetings were held weekly at 10:00 AM. Didn't know what to expect from these introductions. Mr. Rhue introduced me to a roomful of local Swansboro women. I met, Anne Shuller, Amelia Dees-Killet, Betty Faulkner, Colleen Muth, and Mary Katherine Gardner.

The building where the meetings took place was in the former U-shaped Emmerton School and Unitarian church off Church Street. Built-in 1928, it is used today for multiple purposes, including the location of Swansboro's Heritage Center. Inside, it is a mini-museum, full of photographs, artifacts, and lots of cool historical memorabilia. I had arrived where I needed to be, thanks to Mr. Rhue. My journey and quest for facts would become even more interesting.

It was obvious who the woman in charge was. Anne Shuller, a petite eighty-something-year-old woman had an aura about her. Almost like the queen of England, Anne's presence and grace are unmatched. When she spoke, everyone listened. In my head I would name her, 'the Queen of Swansboro.' And when someone talked, they seemed to look for Anne's approval. For an hour or so we drank coffee while discussing upcoming local events like the Pirate Fest for kids and the possibility of doing downtown tours. I soaked in every second of this meeting, even getting in a few questions of my own when the opportunity presented itself.

I assumed this to be a one-week thing. Little did I know that I would attend every Thursday meeting for the next month or two with those wonderful local women of Swansboro at the Heritage Center. They accepted me and allowed me in on their conversations. As a result of my attendance every Thursday, I was also invited to other events held by the Heritage and Historical Society of Swansboro. The book would take on a life on its own at that point. Though Captain Joe Webb was my initial subject, I began to meet the Who's Who of Swansboro. From here on, I knew I had to include reference to the people still with us that were close to Joe's age.

On one Wednesday evening I was invited to a town meeting where an archaeologist from East Carolina named Jimmy Borelli was set to speak. As I took a seat in the back of the room, dozens of people sat in front of me. The topic of the meeting was that of a new artifact donated to the Heritage Center Museum. A huge chunk of tar rosin weighing close to fifty pounds was recently found on a beach in Emerald Isle.

The archaeologist spoke in length about the industry of tar, turpentine, and rosin. He discussed in detail how important the industry was in Swansboro and surrounding areas. Onslow County alone once had over sixty distilleries. At one time we were one of the biggest exporters of the substance to England. It wasn't just the immediate area involved with the industry. Small North Carolina towns like Greenville, Rocky Mount, and Wilson had a hand in the tar business as well. The chunk found had fallen off a ship years ago as it made its way out to sea.

After the meeting, I sparked up conversations with many of the people in attendance. Surprisingly, I knew a handful of people in the room from personal interviews or the Historical Society meetings. A few of the people I didn't know walked up to me and asked about the progress of the book. It surprised me that I was now recognized as part of Swansboro.

I met Andy Ennett, a former mayor of Swansboro in the 1980's. He appeared to be my age and not the seventy-some years old he claimed. I was informed of his former agenda for the town that didn't succeed decades prior. However, much of it has come to fruition today. He seemed to be ahead of his time. I made another friend in the former mayor that evening.

I also met with one of my idols Jack Dudley, the man that has written books about Swansboro. He's old school Swansboro and I've respected him since I was a teenager. Jack is one of Swansboro's most educated locals, earning several degrees from prominent universities, being an engineer for Dupont, and then becoming a dentist. I admitted to him that his book, 'Swansboro –The Friendly City By The Sea,' had been like a Bible to me the previous three months, used daily as a reference and fact checker. For a few minutes, we discussed what I intended to include in my book. At the end of the conversation, we agreed to meet up in a week. I had became rooted in all things Swansboro, so much so that my daily life revolved around writing this book and finding out all that I could about this beautiful small town.

# CHAPTER EIGHT
# WARD CEMETERY

There are numerous aging graveyards spread throughout Swansboro. Their age shows because of the fading tombstones and crooked layout of the plots. There's no true formation. Visitors to the graveyards are forced to walk jig-jagged to avoid stepping on the ones buried there. It's as if there were no original plans in place to bury more than a few individuals or families. Guess as time went on and family members died, they squeezed in as many people as they could. I didn't expect headstones to be lined up in rows like Arlington Cemetery in Washington DC. But I was surprised that visitors had to tread the area carefully and with the greatest of caution.

When I first started writing this book, I occasionally visited several cemeteries in the downtown area. I didn't know what I would find. I simply did this because I knew lots of Swansboro's history was buried with those same people laying at rest there. I wanted to walk among them. I wanted to see the names on the tombstones. I wanted to see when they were born and when they died. That told me the era they lived in and what life might have been like for them. This intrigued me to the core. With complete honesty, when I first did this, they were just names with no personal acknowledgment. I didn't know one name from the next. However, I knew that each had a story and I wanted to find out about as many as I could.

As weeks went by and I continued to tip-toe through the burial sites, last names began to stick out. And as I went on doing interviews and continued my research, certain first names kept on popping up, matching with last names. I also became familiar with not only first and last names but contributions individuals might have made to the community. Additionally, I began to recognize who the parents were to children and visa-versa. The relations and ties to families overwhelmed me. It's like I was getting to know these people that lived before us on a personal level. The more I learned, the more I craved information about the past of Swansboro.

During the period of writing this book, it was not uncommon to see me walking around downtown Swansboro with a backpack on. The backpack usually contained pens, paper, a voice recorder, and the aforementioned Jack Dudley's book on Swansboro. I'd stroll the waterfront, the

side streets, and everything in between. I'd frequently stop at local eateries and stores. There, I always met people and struck up a conversation with them. More often than not, I was told stories about Captain Joe Webb. Even the most unlikely of people knew him. Businessmen from big cities retold stories about Joe. Tourists from the mountains of North Carolina elaborated on their encounters with the fisherman. I would also hear how individuals came to call Swansboro their first or second home. They'd fill me in with their own family's history, what houses they might've grown up in, and their love for this community. I made many friends over many months doing this. And it was all beneficial for the contents of this book.

On one such a walk in the downtown district a while ago, I stopped by the Ward Cemetery at 212 Walnut Street. A huge canopy of oaks and magnolia trees shaded most of the cemetery. Large trees in this area are rare because of the numerous hurricanes that have relentlessly pounded the shores of Swansboro. For some reason, Ward Cemetery didn't seem to have been affected by those same storms. Before I entered, I knew it was about to be a different experience than previous visits. Felt like I was about to enter a church or some other place of religious significance. Not saying it was spiritual but I'm not saying it wasn't either. I stood there for a minute or two, knowing all two-hundred and fifty people lying in rest there had walked the same streets as I did at some point in time. And all two-hundred and fifty people had their own unique story.

As I slowly entered Ward Cemetery, the first headstone I came across would be that of Monte

Hill (1880-1956) and his life partner, Arrilla Piner. Below their names, it read, 'Faithful Parents.' In past visits, Monte Hill was just another name that I randomly came across from time to time. But after months of research, he wasn't just a faithful parent. Monte was a prominent boat builder. Monte was a beloved figure in the community who loved fishing and all things about the sea. He and his business partner Isiah Willis set up shop on Water Street in a place dubbed, 'Poor Man's Hole' or 'Smoky Hollow' after a fire destroyed an old sawmill structure back in the 1930s. The structure, along with sawdust caught ablaze and smoldered, emitting a haze that would persist for months.

For a good twenty-plus years, Monte and Isiah made sea-worthy vessels for the community. They had a hand in building the majority of the boats in Swansboro from the 1930s until the 1950s. I found out that they built over one-hundred boats. Some were as small as twelve feet, while some were as large as fifty feet.

I continued to stroll, coming across numerous last names like the Wards, Hatsell's, Moore's, Furlong's, Bloodgood's, Buckmaster's, Milstead's, Pritchard's, Tolson's, Bell's, Sewell's, Pitman's, Davis's, Dennis's, Woodhull's, Barfield's, Wellspeak's, Keagy's, Privett's, Thomas's, Holloway's, Keel's, Merritt's and one Casper. I now knew each of their last names from interviews I've had and from research. I have met many of their descendants, some even being old friends of mine. I now knew a handful of their stories and in time I knew I would want to know most if not all of them. As I stopped by each one, it hit me how intertwined those families were. Many of the women carried two or three common last names in Swansboro.

Take Mary Ward Pritchard (1878-1955) for example. She was born Mary Moore. Mary's first marriage was to David Ward. After his death, she married Thomas Pritchard. Guess we have to keep in mind how there were very few families around in the late 1800s and early 1900s. It wasn't uncommon for families to marry into other local families frequently. This had to be confusing at family reunions. It's probably safe to say that most small-town families were related to each other in some form or fashion during previous eras.

Each of those family names I mentioned above is still around today except that of the Bloodgoods. Sadly, there are no more Bloodgood last names in Swansboro today, only houses that belonged to them and the stories told about their time in Swansboro. That's another reason why I believe it's important to tell their stories. How does one family's last name disappear altogether?

One of the most recognizable gravesites was that of Tucker Reed Littleton (1936-1983). You may recall this name from my visit to the Archives in Raleigh a few

141

chapters back. He is Swansboro's most cherished historian. If it wasn't for him, most of my research would not have been possible. If it wasn't for him, much of Swansboro's history would be forgotten. Tucker's parents were James Littleton and Neta Parkin Littleton. He was not only a historian, but he was also an ordained minister, teacher, author, linguist, botanist, and scholar. With all those talents, he chose to devote his time to all things Swansboro.

In 1980, Tucker organized a committee to plan the celebration of Swansboro's 200th birthday. He laid the groundwork and secured the funds for the unveiling of the Captain Otway Burns statue in 1983. Swansboro succeeded in celebrating the town's 200th birthday that year, making it a peak year for the seaside village. Sadly, Tucker died a few months later. He left behind a void that can never be filled. He will always be known as the Pride of Swansboro. I hope to see a statue dedicated to him at some point in time. If anyone is deserving of such a distinction, it would be Tucker Littleton. The town does have the Tucker Littleton Visitor's Center at the corner of Water and Church Streets, two doors down from my girlfriend's cottage, that is open to the public. And he does have a plaque near the Captain Otway Burns statue.

Another tombstone that stuck out to me was that of Thomas Merritt Sr. (1854-1932). I remember my friend Billy Parkin telling me about his great-grandfather on his mom's side of the family. And not only is Billy a Merritt on one side of the family, but he is also a Parkin, both common names for the area. Billy told me about his great-grandfather Thomas Merritt Sr. owning property on Water Street. Both the Merritt and Parkin families lived on this street for decades.

Another familiar name I noted was that of Mary Virginia Hill (1873-1945). She too lived on Water Street and would go on to marry James Parkin. What stuck out to me is that three of their daughters named Nellie, Neta, and Bessie married three Littleton brothers who also lived on Water Street. Get this; Neta would birth Tucker Reed Littleton, the same that I mentioned above. I could not imagine in today's time, three daughters marrying three brothers. The dating pool had to be very small.

The oldest tombstone I found belonged to John W.B. Thomas. Born November 21, 1871, but died just a few weeks later. The tombstone itself is faded and cracked in three sections. I researched John W.B. Thomas and could not find out who his parents were.

 I stumbled across a tombstone with a name I had heard over and over, that belonged to Robert Lee Smith (1871-1943). He was mostly known for being Swansboro's most prolific home builder. It's been said that he built up to fifteen houses, the Tarrymore Hotel, and numerous boats. The first home he built was made of salvaged wood from a shipwreck that crashed into

one of the barrier islands called Bear Island. For a few weeks, Smith used a boat to tow the wood he needed across the channel to Swansboro. Years later he would build his permanent residence off Front Street to be near his boatbuilding railway at the end of Main Street. In 1937, Smith finished his last boat named the Valhalla. That's around the same time Monte Hill and Isiah Willis took over the boatbuilding scene. Before Smith was a builder, he was a fisherman, and line boat captain.

During World War I, Smith worked as a carpenter at a Morehead City shipyard, having a hand in building three ships for the war effort. A descendant of  Robert Smith would tell me a neat story about his time in Morehead City during his family's six-month stay there. After each of the three ships was complete, crews and spectators stood around as each vessel was being christened. After a lady broke a bottle of champagne across the bow of the ship, Smith would have the responsibility of cutting the ropes that held it down. The boat would slide into the water with hundreds of people clapping and cheering.

I also found out through the same Robert Smith's descendants that one of the warships he helped build was called Dassalan. At the time, it was the largest ship constructed in North Carolina, measuring 281 feet long, a 28 foot-beam, and a 3,500-ton cargo capacity.

Robert Smith married Lina Russell, another common Swansboro last name. They would have three daughters, Daisy, Amelia, and Marjory. Marjory would live in the Smith house on Front Street until the age of 101. Anne Shuller, the petit lady I got acquainted with at the Historical Society is her daughter, meaning Robert Smith is her grandad. Sadly, Robert Smith died when Anne was very young, and she doesn't have any memories of him. Anne and her husband Bob currently live in the same house her grandparents and mom lived in on Front Street, making it one of the only generational homes left in Swansboro. Amelia Dees-Killet, another woman I met at the Historical Society is the granddaughter of Amelia Smith, making her and Anne cousins. Amelia Smith married a Canady, the same family as Jim Canady, the man Joe Webb found floating in the water back in 1947. Both Anne Shuller and Amelia Dees-Killet are also related to the Moore's and the Russel's.

I also came across Charles Webb's (1873-1851) headstone, Joe's grandad. Not too far from him lay Captain Joe Webb's parents, Horace (1914-1958) and Katherine Webb (1915-2003). Katherine remarried after Horace's death. Officially she was known as Katherine Fields Meadows Webb Pittman, another local lady with multiple last names common for the area. Beside them lays Joe's sister that he named his boat after, Anna Webb Sermons (1935-1961). Horace owned H.J. Grocery and several other businesses which he would run until the time of his death. Because of Horace and Katherine's hard work, Captain Joe Webb and his family would eventually inherit property that Captain Otway Burns once owned.

As a side note, that day I was at The Ward Cemetery, numerous men were there cleaning up. They represented workers for the town of Swansboro. One even asked me if I needed help in finding a particular gravesite. What a sincere gesture. I wondered if the town had always maintained the grounds. From further research, I found out that Billy Underseth, that man whose family once owned the Green House, the oldest house in Swansboro, was the Ward Cemetery's caretaker from 1960-1988. He cut the grass, cleared debris after storms, and always made sure flowers that people left behind by loved ones' headstones were always upright.

I knew there would be many more personal visits to Ward's Cemetery and other graveyards in and around Swansboro before the conclusion of the book. I wanted to know more about each person that is buried in the local cemeteries and to learn more about Swansboro in the process.

# CHAPTER NINE
# MORTON'S ACADEMY AND THE
# MILITARY

After word got around Swansboro about my intentions of writing the book with Captain Joe Webb, I received another interesting message from a young local named Josh Wells. Josh claimed that his grandad and great-uncle had a museum on their property outside downtown Swansboro. He said it was an old school called Morton's Academy. I had never heard of it nor had any of my friends for that matter. Intrigued, I followed up the lead and decided to pay Josh and his family a visit. I didn't expect to find much there. Boy, was I in for one of my biggest surprises yet?

With the directions Josh had given me, I parked in the driveway of a one-story brick house off the Main Street extension. Josh immediately came outside to greet me. Two older gentlemen and a woman followed close behind him. As far as my eyes could see, I couldn't see any standing building that resembled a school or an academy nearby. I met Josh's grandad named Bobby Wells and his towering great-uncle in Norman Wells. The first thing I noticed was their hard handshakes. Their vice-like grips were a real man's handshake. It had been years since anyone has shaken my hand that hard. I was already a fan of theirs. Faye, Josh's grandmother was polite and cordial but not much with words.

I was then led behind several houses that belonged to the family. An older white building suddenly appeared. Josh was right. His family had a freaking museum in the back of their yards. While walking, Josh's grandad gave me a rundown of the property. It had been in their family for over seventy years. The white building, Morton Academy was moved a mile from its original location in 1996 to their land. After the complete restoration of the school in 2013 in commemoration of teachers and students of Morton's Academy, it opened up to the public, thanks to brothers Bobby, Norman, and Clayton Wells.

Before entering the 140-year-old wooden structure, we took several pictures together and spoke at length about what I was going to do with the information I possibly found. I knew whatever I came across would land in the book in some form. Just didn't know how I could fit in at that particular moment. Just like Joe Rhue, I made friends with Norman, Bobby, and Faye Wells. From their hospitality, it felt as if I was already a Wells family member. The old-school mentality and community spirit run prevalent in these parts. I couldn't wait to enter Morton's Academy.

We passed the tall outdoor school bell and then climbed the short wooden staircase leading up to the entrance. My breath was nearly taken away when stepping inside. Not only were antique school desks lined up in neat rows, but mannequins dressed up as students sat behind them, giving it the complete feel of the early 1900s. The attire of each student was that of an earlier era. I sat down on a bench and soaked it all in. Meanwhile, to make the experience more authentic, Bobby played a prerecorded voiceover

set up for visitors.

At the front of the classroom, the mannequin of former teacher, Mrs. Daisy Moore stood over her class. The prerecorded voice belonged to her. She spoke to Morton Academy visitors, making me feel as if I was among the dozens of students. For minutes, she went on detailing facts about her and the school's routine. -The one-room schoolhouse was used from 1880-1920. -Along with her students, she had to walk miles to school every day.

The outside bell was rung at 9:00 AM to let the students know the class was going to start. Grades 1-8 attended the school. Boys had to sit on the right side of the classroom. Girls sat on the left. Before class began, they recited the Pledge of Allegiance and said the Lord's Prayer. The school was not held during harvest time, as children were expected to help in the fields. Eighth-grade students assisted the younger students with reading assignments. A handbell on the desk was rung by Miss Daisy after recess. The school concluded at 4:00 PM. The voiceover ceased.

We learned about Daisy Smith Moore earlier. She was one of Robert Smith's three daughters. That would make her Anne Shuller's aunt. I had spoken with Anne earlier that week about all three Smith sisters, mostly about Daisy. Anne shared with me a story about her Aunt Daisy that will put life in perspective for each of us. After finishing high school, Daisy was accepted to East Carolina Teachers College, now known as East Carolina University in Greenville, North Carolina.

Today, we can jump in our car and make the short trip from Swansboro to Greenville in about an hour and a half. Wasn't that easy for Miss Daisy. Her trek would be much more arduous. First, she had to take a slow freight boat from Swansboro to Morehead City. That took about five hours. From there, she rode on a horse and buggy to New Bern. That took well over eight hours. Finally, Miss Daisy took a train to Greenville, adding a few more hours to her long trip. Altogether, the journey to East Carolina Teachers College took close to twenty-four hours.

I walked around the old schoolhouse, staring at the over one-hundred-year-old memorabilia. Norman and Bobby took every step with me.

Every time I paused to gaze at an item, they told me how they stumbled across it. Old textbooks filled the shelves. Old photographs hung on the walls. The museum even had a bucket of playing marbles sitting in a corner. I remember Captain Joe Webb telling me that marbles was once his favorite game in grade school. Keep in mind, he grew up in the generation after the Morton Academy closed down in 1920. Nowadays, toys are outdated after a few years. Marbles appeared to be a popular toy for several generations of our youth.

There was also a heating furnace in the center of the classroom to help keep the students and Miss Daisy warm in the wintertime. I had forgotten that they didn't have electricity. Had to be cold in the winter, furnace or no furnace, and toasty when the weather warmed up with no air-conditioner. I asked Bobby and Norman how they might've kept cool. Norman opened up a second door, allowing a light breeze to come through. I could only imagine what the students and the teacher had to deal with.

Let's not forget what they had to do when needing to use the bathroom since there was no plumbing. I'm sure an outhouse of some sort had been nearby. There was however a small hand pump water well in the back of the classroom. Norman saw me looking at it and stepped in front of me. With a few pumps, water trickled out. Made me think how far society had come in terms of the advancement of technology.

The brothers had done a magnificent job in restoring Morton's Academy. Took me back to the early 1900s for the short time I was there. They had done Swansboro and history justice with efforts to preserve this school. They are keepers of our past. I thanked them immensely for their time and promised to stay in touch with them. I didn't know how I would work my experience with them in the book, but I knew it would become part of it. Before leaving, their vice-like grips shook my hand as I said goodbye to the new friends that I had made.

Right before I got into my car I looked back at Josh and said, "This will be yours one day. Do what you got to do to keep this thing going. This is part of your family's legacy."

I stowed away the notes I had taken about Morton's Academy and went on learning and writing about other facets of Swansboro, keeping Bobby and Norman in my heart for what they had done with the school. For weeks my daily routine consisted of waking up around 5:30, chugging tons of coffee, typing on the computer, searching for unseen photos for the book, and then taking a walk-in downtown Swansboro. Some days I ran into Joe. We might've talked in length about a subject, or we just said hello. I set up at least three interviews every week with people that reached out. Some I had contacted because another person referred them to me. Many times, I imbibed new information about Swansboro or Captain Joe Webb. In a few of the interviews, I learned nothing new but either way, I enjoyed those encounters. It was never a waste of my time.

I returned to the Well's property a month

later. It wasn't actually to ask more questions about what I had learned from them and about Morton's Academy. Mainly, I wanted to sit down with Norman and Bobby to talk to my new friends and to check in on them. With these types of interactions, you never know what perhaps could come out of it. We sat in Bobby's living room, the décor from decades earlier. I began sharing with them what I had learned so far about past events and the people of Swansboro. They seemed to be interested in what I found. As I went on, they lit up.

Norman would say something like, 'Oh, I remember that.' And then he would add details to the story that I wasn't aware of. I pulled out my pen and paper and scribbled notes down as fast as I possibly could. I'd change the subject and then it would be Bobby saying, 'I know who you are talking about.' They filled the gaps in the stories where they needed it. They didn't know how much this helped me. We sat there for an hour, going back and forth, and talking about fishing, farming, and the military. The latter is a segway for what I wanted to get into next.

You may recall in the introduction chapter I spoke about the presence of the military here and how we often hear planes, helicopters, and the sounds of bombs consistently being dropped. It wasn't always like that on the Crystal Coast. Because of the numerous armies clashing in Europe and the Japanese navy making a move in the Pacific Ocean during the early 1940s, the United States decided to devise a plan in case they were drawn into war.

In 1941, Major John McQueen was directed to, 'select a pilot, get a plane, and find us a training center.' For six weeks, he flew from Corpus Christi, Texas up to Norfolk, Virginia in search of a location. He would choose a 14-mile stretch of pristine beaches that were mostly undeveloped in Onslow County, North Carolina, just fifteen miles south of Swansboro.

In less than six months, construction would begin on the world's largest amphibious training center. The 110,000 acres the military chose were not uninhabited. There were homes, churches, cemeteries, and businesses present. And there were also farms and fishing villages. The federal government invoked eminent domain on the 720 families that called the area home. Land acquisition began immediately. The military gave the families three months to vacate their property between June 1, 1941 and September 1, 1941.

The power and priorities of the War Department overtook the concern of the citizens. The families were somewhat financially compensated, but it wasn't enough for them to purchase a comparable home. My research suggests it often took years before many of the families were given a dime. I read that the federal government only paid 1.5 million for the 110,000 acres. The abuse of those families was largely overlooked after the Japanese attacked Pearl Harbor. The land takeover was deemed essential; training the largest military the United States ever had. On the brink of World War II, the Marines would call Camp Lejeune in Jacksonville, North Carolina home.

The establishment of Camp Lejeune would

change the face of Onslow County, including Swansboro. Because of our natural resources, low population, and remote islands, the area was a perfect fit for the Marines to perform large maneuvers and artillery firing. In 1943, Jacksonville became a boomtown, with military housing and developments popping up everywhere and Marine families flocking here from around the country.

The Wells family flourished with the military's growth. Camp Lejuene needed craftsmen, carpenters, and other professionals to work on the large base. Their dad, Elwood Wells was a private contractor for the military. I was told Elwood farmed in the daytime and did electrical work on base at night. By the 1950s, the government employed approximately 22,000 people. As a relative comparison, the population of Onslow County in the 1940s was less than 20,000. Today, well over 210,000 citizens call Onslow County home. Most live in the city of Jacksonville or close to it.

Downtown Swansboro remains pretty much intact, but the outskirts are full of cookie-cutter housing developments, stretching out for miles and miles. As a result of the expanding military in the area, Swansboro surrendered its isolation and a small-town feel in exchange for tax dollar prosperity and explosion of population growth. The rest is history. Bombs, live ammunition, planes, and helicopters are a big part of our everyday lives.

WHEREINTHEHELLIS
SWANSBORO
NORTH CAROLINA
For Charter
BILLY ANNA
CAPT.
JOE WEBB PH.

# CHAPTER TEN
## TALES FROM THE TABLE AND SEA

Captain Joe hadn't been feeling well for a few weeks, so when I would see him, I didn't question him about past events or his family. His days were filled with periodic doctor visits. I didn't want to burden him too much with memories. I did however request to go out on the Billy Anna II once he was feeling better. I was anxious to go out on the boat with him. My visits were brief during these few weeks, sometimes just staying for less than five minutes. Joe seemed to enjoy the company and I absolutely got personal satisfaction from checking in on the man I had come to call my godfather.

Nevertheless, I was still able to learn more about him from other people. From interviewing four of his former first mates, I was told story after story of Captain Joe and his days out at sea. Those men's experiences with him provided memories that would last a lifetime. I learned from them that Captain Joe wasn't just their boss. He was a friend, mentor, and teacher. I was reminded that Captain Joe is kind-hearted, daring, adventurous, and sometimes reckless individual.

Captain Joe has a natural desire to share his experiences with other people. I'm told that when a charter had children on board, Captain Joe loved to educate those kids. Take floating Sargasso grass for example. The seaweed-looking stuff can often be seen while at sea. Lots of fishermen look for it because schools of fish usually congregate beneath the scattered grass. Lots of times, if you locate the grass, fish will come soon thereafter.

So, when fishing slowed down considerably, Joe would hang one of his arms off the side of the boat and scoop up a handful of the Sargasso grass. Next, he laid the contents on the floor of his vessel, kneeled with the kids, and described to them what was hidden among the grass like plankton, microscopic shrimp, and sea horses. He explained that the floating grass was Mother Nature's way of restocking the ocean. Just a little biology lesson from Joe to make the trip worthwhile to the customers and to hopefully educate our youth.

Many people complain about the Sargasso grass once it hits the shore, but most don't know the importance of it. They believe it to just be seaweed. Of course, I didn't know better either until finding out from Captain Joe's first mates.

Many of Captain Joe's first mates initially questioned some of the tales they had heard about Captain Joe Webb, but once they went out in the ocean with him, they became a part of other legendary stories that would have been hard for the average person to believe.

Like one time Captain Joe was talking to customers while at the helm and not paying attention to his surroundings at Bear Inlet. In doing so, Billy Anna II accidentally ran aground, puncturing a hole at the bottom of the boat. Acting quickly, Joe got the vessel running at top speed to limit the amount of seawater seeping in.

On the way back to shore, he radioed Dudley's Marina about his situation. An employee named Jerry Jones rushed to his house to retrieve a set of rails to be used for when or if Joe even made it back. With water pouring over the stern and up to the customer's knees, Captain Joe traveled through the inlets twice as fast as any other nearby boat. The people on land and the other boats knew something was wrong. To see Captain Joe Webb going that fast through the inlets, there had to be some kind of trouble or imminent danger. I'm told hundreds of people witnessed this particular incident.

By the time Dudley's Marina came into sight, Jerry Jones had laid the railings a few feet into the water for the sinking boat. The vessel had to hit it just right for this maneuver to work and for the boat to be landed. The twin diesel engines on board made all kinds of grunts and whines as they inched closer and closer. The drenched customers and first-mate held on for dear life. At least if the Billy Anna II did sink, they wouldn't have had to swim very far. Aimed just right, the boat centered the rails. With all the concentration he had in him, Captain Joe hit those rails perfectly and kept the boat safe from sinking. Once on land, the customers, first mate, and Captain Joe were all smiles. Just another day at the office for Billy Anna II.

It took a month to repair the damaged hull before the Billy Anna II became seaworthy again.

I'm told those same customers have kept in contact with Joe over the years. Additionally, three other incidents similar to the one you just read occurred over fifteen years. The story above was Joe's fault. He will be the first to admit it. The others he blames on other people and various circumstances.

I had the honor of another old friend of Joe's reaching out to me. Through Facebook, I asked him questions about Joe and Swansboro. I couldn't ignore what he wrote. After reading it, I knew the letter had to be shared.

Tom Lehman writes:

*'As I was getting to know Joe, I wasn't sure if he was making his experiences up, greatly exaggerating, or if there was some truth in what he was saying. Turns out, they were true. Spend time with him on any vessel, especially the Billy Anna II and you would know exactly what I mean. I have fished several parts of the United States as well as internationally, and I have not met anyone who knows and respects the ocean more than him.'*

*'I have spent more time with Joe at sea than on land. As such, many memories come from our time together on the water. He shared the knowledge he had developed from decades and countless hours on the ocean. Joe taught me how to navigate without the aid of electronics or compasses. Believe it or not, a person can quickly determine their approximate location on the water by observing the path of airplanes above on sunny days.'*

*'Joe fished when anglers did not have coordinates to run to in search of a productive day*

*of fishing. Instead, he built mental images of those spots through the tools he used and the knowledge he had accumulated. I was driven to fish with Joe as often as I could. I wanted to learn more about what he knew. On days that Joe was unable to join fishing expeditions, he would meet us at the dock beforehand and afterward. In the mornings, we discussed the places we should target. This is when I learned Joe's view of the ocean is different from anyone I have ever met and was built upon a complex mental image of what was beneath the ocean's surface. He might tell us to "run out there about twenty-five minutes until you hit the hard bottom rocky area, then turn southeast along a two-mile stretch of the sandy bottom until you hit a spot of deeper water with a big area of rocks." I would spend days trying to recreate Joe's mental imagery without success. However, when he got on the boat and explained his directions, what he was saying was correct as validated with the electronics on whatever boat we were fishing on. When Joe was on the boat, we caught more fish. Period.'*

*'Joe enjoys fishing tournament days whether he is fishing in the tournament or not. Everyone who fishes the tournaments locally knows Joe as a legend and his unique voice is very distinguishable even at sea across radio networks. One day during the Swansboro Bluewater Tournament when fishing became slow, Joe serenaded the tournament fleet with a performance of Pinky Lee (1950's sitcom) across the tournament channel to the joy of all!'*

*'Visiting Joe's house is better than visiting any*

maritime museum. You will find many artifacts and photos of a young Joe which chronicle his time growing up where he would revolutionize fishing forever on the Crystal Coast. Joe fished before modern electronics were available to mariners and anglers. Joe has several rolls of Reel Paper, very similar to the paper that comes from cash registers which I took note of. The Reel Paper came from old sonar devices which reported the density of the ocean floor by recording lines on the paper representing sandy versus rocky surfaces. This method allowed Joe to build to own collection of productive fishing areas that he would leverage in his charter business. He is a walking body of knowledge, and I was eager to learn.'

'One summer day, Joe asked me to join him at an oyster and pig roast in Cedar Point. We arrived at a spirited party at a great place his dear friend Martin owned. Joe knew several people at the party who quickly informed him that the keg was holding what they referred to as sipping beer. Joe responded with a rapid, unfiltered response, "Well that's no good because I like to chug my beer." Good times were had.'

'Swansboro is a special place that is home to this larger-than-life gentleman. It's also a better place to have Joe as a resident, fixture, and representative. He has made many positive impacts on my life that I am forever grateful for. When I learned of the book Chad was creating, I was thrilled and felt compelled to contribute to the legacy of this wonderful man who has influenced my life and the life of so many others in so many ways.'

-Tom Lehman

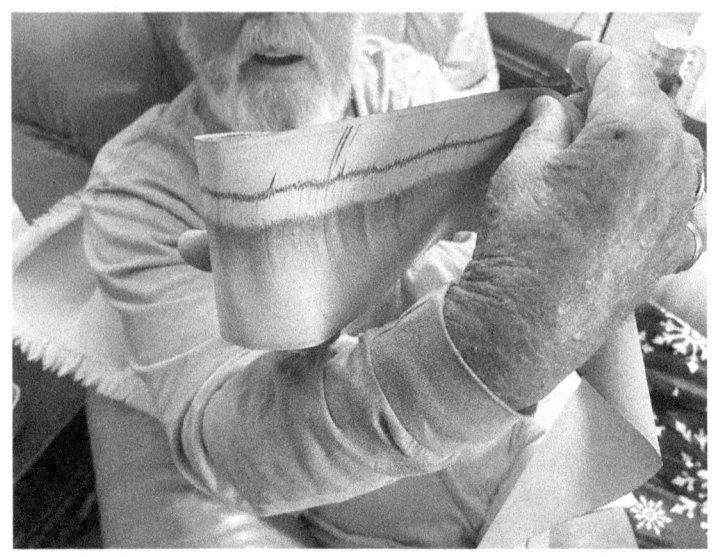

*Captain Joe Webb holding Reel Paper mapping
the bottom of the ocean*

I remember on top of some tall tales and stories, I also heard all about some of Joe's quirks. One was that of him eating other people's food. My mom once told me that they were at this big fancy dinner one night and Joe stopped a passing waiter with a large tray of food. Joe grabbed a few pieces of shrimp off it and commented, 'They aren't bad at all.'

Dumbfounded, the waiter continued to the intended table where the food was to be delivered and admitted to the customers what Joe had done. A lady at the same table stormed up to Joe and confronted him. Mom assumed it to be an accident and took up for him, almost getting into a physical altercation with the lady. In a heated argument, they made a big scene in the restaurant, forcing everyone to stop what they were doing.

I thought that was a one-time occurrence but two of his former first mates admitted that Joe helped himself to the food of paying charters on the Billy Anna II on multiple occasions. I'm told that those same customers would look at Joe incredulously as he ate to his heart's content out of their coolers. The whole time he carried that schoolboy grin he's always been known to have.

Another time, full of booze, he sat at a bar of a local restaurant drinking after a long day out on the water. A family sat behind him, eating their dinner. Joe staggered to their table, grabbed some of their appetizers, put the food in his mouth, and said to them, 'I want to thank you, guys, for coming in.' Finally, he stumbled back to the bar as if eating other people's food was normal.

Though the above isn't what a model citizen's behavior looks like, I'm told some heartfelt stories out on the ocean that didn't include him eating other people's food. One such charter had nine-year-old twin boys on board with their father. After they were miles out in the Atlantic Ocean, one of the twins got seasick and threw up his breakfast from the side of the boat. Joe slowed down to allow the youngster to finish and compose himself. When the boat went into idle, the other twin began laughing and mocking his sick brother. Joe witnessed the father do nothing to comfort his sick son or to stop the other brother from laughing and mocking his twin.

Captain Joe climbed down the tower and checked on the one that was sick. He gave him some water and then handed over a towel so the nine-year-old could wipe his face. After the boy appeared to be okay, the captain turned to the other boy and said, 'You see your brother? You have to always look after him. He is going to always be your twin brother. You love and respect him, because if you don't other people will laugh and mock him. Do you want people to laugh and mock you?' The boy shook his head 'no.'

Captain Joe climbed back up the tower, got behind the wheel, and continued towards the warm waters of the Gulfstream. Less than an hour later, the twin that laughed and mocked his brother was leaning over the edge of the boat, heaving up his breakfast. Joe brought the vessel to another stop. He peered over at the sick boy, waiting for the father to look after his son. In a heartfelt gesture, the brother who was sick earlier gave his newly sick twin brother a bottle of water and a clean towel to wipe his mouth and face. Hopefully, Captain Joe Webb taught those twins a lesson that day in always having each other's back. I felt warm and fuzzy after hearing the above story.

I do have another similar story with a different outcome. Joe picked up a charter, one morning in the summer of 2000. The customers were a bunch of men from New York. Before departing, the men complained about numerous things and talked down to Joe and his first mate. Joe tried to make the best of the situation by telling jokes. Once they got out into deep waters, the griping continued. Not only were they complaining, but they were also rude, making snide comments and being very demanding. Captain Joe and his first mate could only exchange glances of, 'What in the world have we gotten ourselves into?'

Before the first mate had the opportunity to bait the lines, one of the men got seasick and started throwing up. Joe slowed the boat down for him as he did with the twin brothers. Then, one after another, each man leaned over the railing on the Billy Anna II and heaved their guts out. Joe and his first mate exchanged smiles. This went on for minutes before Joe yelled down to them, 'That ought to get some of the Yankee out of ya's!' That story made me laugh.

There was another time Captain Joe took a charter out for a man that was supposed to be some oilfield bigwig from Texas. It was a successful day, catching fish after fish. Soon as a line was in the water, a fish immediately hooked on. It was just one of those beautiful days out on the water with Captain Joe. After a good hour or so, the oilman from Texas demanded, 'I got an extra five-hundred bucks if we catch a Billfish.'

Joe idled the boat, barked out what type of bait to use for the first mate, and then full throttled the Billy Anna II to an area known as the Swansboro Hole. Once there, the lines went out a hundred yards trailing behind them. In seconds, a monster fish had been hooked. Joe yelled out, 'Got another one in the sock!'

A gigantic Blue Marlin with large fins suddenly leaped out of the water. The oilman reeled and reeled for a good hour, giving the man the fight of his life. Joe angled the boat just right every few minutes. The first mate gave instructions to the customer when to ease up and when to reel to tire out the Blue Marlin. Pretty soon, the humongous fish was beside the boat. Guess with all the adrenaline running through the oilman, the customer said, 'I got another thousand bucks if we get it on board.'

Joe stopped the boat, leaned down, and told him, 'We don't break the rules. We might catch these types of fish but this one ain't long enough to keep. You won't like eating these fish, mister. They got dark meat. You can take a picture if you want. And by the way, you owe my first mate that five-hundred dollars.' That's Joe for you, doing the right thing and looking after his first mate.

From each of the first mates I spoke to, they loved the man dearly. Not one bad word was said about him other than him being occasionally frugal. Above are only a handful of stories. Think about this. Joe chartered nearly 150 customers a year. Now multiply that by fifty years of service. That's 7, 500 charters. And that is 7,500 different stories and experiences with Captain Joe Webb and Billy Anna.

Even though I couldn't pepper Joe with

questions during those few weeks, I did visit the Archives in Raleigh three more times doing extensive research on Swansboro. The drive seemed shorter every time. And each time I came to Raleigh, I stumbled across great restaurants and other places open to the public. Within a few blocks of the Archives, I also visited the North Carolina Museum of Natural Sciences, the Museum of History, the Governor's Mansion, and the State Capitol. There is a ton to do for both kids and adults in that immediate vicinity. The streets of Raleigh were clean and appeared relatively safe.

I do have a suggestion for you, the reader. No matter where you are from, I recommend visiting your local or state Archives. It's a cool experience just being able to go through boxes full of the history of your hometown. You never know what you may find. Almost feels like you are snooping in on someone's diary. I'll admit, some of it might be boring but once you find information you never knew or locate old photos, the feeling is exhilarating. Some of the photos you see in this book are from my trips to the Archives. Probably cost me three or four dollars for a reprint. Worth every penny of it. Even if you are from a small town, go see what is there. Might even be something you could do with your family. Your tax dollars pay for it so why not utilize it? After completing this book, I plan to visit the Archives and downtown Raleigh area every chance I can.

# CHAPTER ELEVEN
# SWANSBORO'S BUSINESS DISTRICT

During the midst of research, interviews, and working on the contents of the book, I paid a visit to The Poor Man's Hole antique store two or three times a week to see Mr. Rhue. It was almost mandatory to swing by when I walked downtown. We didn't just talk about Swansboro; we spoke of our families and other events going on in the world. As I said before, I made a new friend in Mr. Rhue.

I loved the way he looked at life, never really taking anything too seriously. His lighthearted nature would be contagious. Mr. Rhue demanded that I call him Joe. So, I did in person but for the sake of not confusing you with him and Joe Webb, I refer to him as Mr. Rhue throughout the book. If you ever get a chance to meet the man, call him Joe. That's his preference.

During my walks in Swansboro, I frequented many other establishments on Front Street as well. In many of these places, I met and spoke with the present owners and their employees. By that time, I had learned so much about each building in downtown Swansboro from Captain Joe and from other inquiries. I began to know what businesses were there before the current ones and would share it with the owners if they

| BOILED HARD CRABS | | FRIED HARD CRABS | | DEVIL CRAB IN SHELL | |
|---|---|---|---|---|---|
| With Drawn Butter | | $1.75 | | $2.25 | |
| $1.75 | | | | | |

| CRAB CAKES | | CRAB MEAT | |
|---|---|---|---|
| $2.00 | | Au Gratin | |
| | | $3.25 | |

| Soft Shell Crabs | | Devil Crab Casserole | | Lump Crabmeat In Butter | |
|---|---|---|---|---|---|
| Large Order | 3.25 | Large Order | 2.25 | Large Order | 3.25 |
| Small Order | 2.75 | Small Order | 1.75 | Small Order | 2.75 |

All Served With French Fries — Cole Slaw — Hush Puppies

| Golden Special Brown Fried **CHICKEN DINNERS** | | **FROG LEGS** | | CHARCOAL BROILED U.S. CHOICE WESTERN **T-Bone Steaks** | |
|---|---|---|---|---|---|
| ½ Chicken | $1.75 | LARGE ORDER (Approx. 4 Pr.) | 4.50 | | |
| ¼ CHICKEN | $1.25 | SMALL ORDER (Approx. 2 Pr.) 2.50 | | SMALL — (12 to 14 oz.) | 3.50 |
| Served With Tomato Juice French Fries — Cole Slaw Hot Rolls & Butter | | Served With Fresh Green Toss Salad French Fries Hot Rolls & Butter | | MEDIUM — (16 to 18 oz.) | 4.50 |
| | | | | LARGE — (20 to 24 oz.) | 5.50 |
| Creamed Potatoes & Brown Gravy 50c Extra | | | | Served With French Fries or Cheese Potato & Fresh Green Toss Salad, Hot Rolls & Butter | |

| Thick Center Cut **HAM STEAK** $2.00 | Hickory Smoked Pork **BARBEQUE** $2.00 |
|---|---|
| Served With Pineapple Ring or Apple Sauce, Cole Slaw — French Fries — Rolls or Hush Puppies — | Served With French Fries — Cole Slaw And Hush Puppies |

**SOUPS**

| CLAM CHOWDER | 1.00 | OYSTER STEW (Plain or Milk) | 1.50 | SCALLOP STEW | 1.50 |
|---|---|---|---|---|---|

| Plates For Children Under 12 Years Only $1.25 | | **BEVERAGES** | | **SIDE ORDERS** | |
|---|---|---|---|---|---|
| | | COFFEE | .10 | CHEESE POTATOES | .25 |
| You may select either one or two Seafoods listed under Combinations of your choice, Fried Chicken, Ham Steak or Barbeque. Slaw & French Fries. | | SANKA per cup | .15 | CREAMED POTATOES | .25 |
| | | HOT TEA per cup | .15 | FRENCH FRIES | .25 |
| | | ICE COFFEE per glass | .20 | GREEN TOSS SALAD | .50 |
| | | ICE TEA | .15 | COLE SLAW | .15 |
| | | MILK Sm—.15 Lg | .25 | FRIED ONION RINGS | .75 |
| All dinners that are not specified "Broiled" or "Saute" will be 50c extra. | | COKE .20 7-Up | .20 | RAW ONION RINGS | .25 |
| | | GINGER ALE | .25 | SLICED TOMATOES | .25 |
| | | COLLINS MIX | .50 | COCKTAIL SAUCE | .15 |
| | | ICE SET UPS | .75 | DRAWN BUTTER | .15 |
| | | | | APPLE SAUCE | .15 |
| Extra Place Setting | 1.00 | ICE BUCKET | .50 | **Desserts** | |
| | | ICE-GLASS & LEMON | .15 | CREAM LEMON PIE | .25 |
| | | | | SHERBET | .20 |

Inside of the Original Captain Charlie's Restaurant Menu - 1958

381

didn't know. Just like how I got familiar with first and last names by visiting graveyards, I got to know the history of Swansboro's infrastructure by visiting and researching each building.

Take the present-day Swansboro Food & Beverage Company for example. The restaurant has one of the best brunches in town. It is in the same building where Captain Charlie's Restaurant used to be, named after Charlie Buckmaster Sr. That restaurant opened in the late 1950s but Charlie died shortly thereafter. His business partner, Durwood Aman took over and was successful for many years. Charlie's was known to have some of the tastiest seafood around. Before Captain Charlie's Restaurant, it was known as the Swan Café owned by Mabel Gerock. The parking lot of Swansboro Food & Beverage Company is where the Tarrymore Hotel was located, and it was Swan Café during that era that catered to the hotel's visitors.

The once-standing two-story Tarrymore Hotel had 24 rooms and a huge, covered porch that faced the White Oak River. The owner, William J. Moore hired Robert Smith as his master carpenter. Finished in 1911, the establishment would be a Swansboro landmark from the early 1920s to the mid-1940s. It wasn't just a place to stay overnight for visitors that fished and hunted. It was also a social hub and dancehall complete with a jukebox on the aforementioned porch for the locals.

Saturday nights were considered the big night for teenagers and young adults. Before the construction of Highway 24, the Tarrymore Hotel had a long wooden walkway that led to a gazebo on the White Oak River which  the locals dubbed 'the love nest.' It's said many couples made out in the love nest and I can't forget to mention the numerous marriage proposals the gazebo witnessed.

The hotel turned into an apartment building in the 1950s, bringing the hotel's heyday to a close. A non-local purchased Captain's Charlie's Restaurant and the apartments in the 1960s. At that time, Highway 24 was widened by the state of North Carolina, the road coming very close to the apartment complex. The days were numbered for the once-popular hotel and social hub. The town needed this expansion due to the ever-growing traffic throughout the area. Sadly, the owner eventually tore down the structure and made it into a parking lot for his restaurant, leaving Swansboro with only pictures and memories of the Tarrymore Hotel.

Across the street from Swansboro Food & Beverage Company is the old Mattock's House and the miniature-sized Dorothy Sander's Café directly beside it. William 'Willie' Mattocks, a merchant marine and engineer, teamed up with Robert Smith in 1901 to build this house. The

Mattock's House is now a popular Airbnb because of its location and scenic views. The former Dorothy Sander's Café, built around 1940 with attributes similar to Mattock's House, used to be a teahouse, catering to travelers along Highway 24 after the state widened its roads. William Mattock's daughter, Ida Barnum 'Dollie' Mattocks operated the tea house. The small building is currently run as The Mustard Seed Boutique, a store with women's apparel, jewelry, and other knick-knacks.

Next to the old Mattock's House is The Boro Restaurant and Bar, a property owned and operated by Randy Swanson. Before The Boro Restaurant and Bar, it was known as the Icehouse Restaurant, an eatery that operated successfully for decades. The Icehouse Restaurant was named after the original use of the building. Back in the 1920s, a guy named Steve Milsted built Swansboro's first icehouse there. No longer did locals have to travel to Morehead City or Jacksonville for ice. Keep in mind, these were the days when most people didn't have refrigerators. Captain Joe admitted that Steve Milstead shared information with him about commercial refrigeration, that he would utilize for his own grocery store and meat market.

The outdoor eating area of The Boro Restaurant and Bar is where live bands play for patrons. The actual stage is the very foundation where a former well-received 'jukebox joint' once stood called Codfish, owned and operated by R.L. Williams Sr. Codfish was a bar complete with pool tables and an impromptu dance floor. In the 1936 movie, 'Captain January,' Shirley Temple and Buddy Ebsen performed a song and dance called, 'At the Codfish Ball.' Guess during those times, it was a popular dance. The Codfish Bar borrowed that name from the movie.

I've asked Captain Joe about the Codfish but since the bar was open before his time, he didn't have any personal stories to tell me. Frustratingly, there are no locals alive that were around when

the Codfish was open. There are rumors about the Codfish era being some wild and crazy times. Lots of drunken fishermen, that sort of thing. I do have something to share with you. In a photo included, you will see Captain Joe holding a light brown beer mug that came from Codfish. The beer mug is nearly one hundred years old, given to Joe by an old friend in R.L. Williams Jr, the Codfish owner's son. What a piece of history! I'd seen the mug in his house numerous times but not once asked about it. I can only imagine the items Joe has collected over the years.

Catty-corner and on the opposite side of the street from The Boro Restaurant and Bar, you will find Dini's Martinis and Desserts in the old Mclean building. Dini's is an upscale bar, a popular date night destination for locals and tourists. The décor is old-world Chicago style, full of cool relics from the gangster days of Al Capone during the 1920s and 1930s. This brings me to a neat story detailing the actual bar inside. For those of you of a certain age, you may remember the iconic talk show host, Geraldo Riveria. Back in the 1980's he had a special segment for his show where he was at the old Lexington Hotel in Chicago, Illinois. It was rumored that Al Capone hung out there in the 1920s and 30s. It's also said he had a hidden safe, full of valuables, in that same hotel.

In Geraldo's special live segment, he knocked down a wall where the safe was thought to be hidden. It ended up being a big nothingburger, but millions of people watched, giving Geraldo a record number of ratings even though nothing turned up. The Lexington Hotel eventually closed down. The actual large wooden bar that was in that hotel is the same one at Dini's Martinis and Desserts, shipped in four pieces from Chicago to Swansboro. Just envision Al Capone sitting at the same bar, drinking his favorite alcoholic beverage. Dini's Martinis is a smash hit for Swansboro.

The current owners of Dini's Martinis and Desserts are Todd and Emily Dini, whose presence is there nearly every night. Todd is also known as a local photographer. Some of his recent photos capture beautiful shots of the immediate area that are sometimes caught with a drone. From sunrises, and sunsets, to the blossoming of the sunflowers at the foot of the Emerald Isle Bridge, his pictures always come back looking like an oil canvassed painting.

The building Dini's Martinis is in was built in 1847 by a man named Robert Spence Mclean. From reading Jack Dudley's book, I learned that during the Civil War, the Yankees ransacked the Mclean building when it had a general store inside of it. Over the ensuing years, the building has served as a pharmacy and a grocery store. I also learned from Captain Joe that his father Horace bought the Mclean building in 1933. Horace ran H.J. Webb grocery for years from the Mclean building before turning it into the town's first over-the-counter drug store. He would sell the Mclean building to Mamie Piner. Mamie ran Seafarers Restaurant in the building in the late 1940's and late 1950's.

That leads me to that building directly beside it, which is often referred to as the 'Russel Old Tyme Shoppe'. This building was constructed in 1916. In 1947, Horace purchased the building and ran a grocery store and meat market for years. As a side and comical note, when Joe took over the meat market after his father's death, the store's slogan was, 'Can't beat Webb's meat.' Only Captain Joe Webb.

Before H.J. Webb's Grocery the establishment was known as Wade's Theatre, the first motion picture theater in Swansboro. David Wade bought the property from Joe Foster in 1943. For a good four years, Wade's Theatre played movies and would be the go-to place for kids. Admission was 50 cents for adults and 15 cents for children. Joe added some fun facts about the place. At the time the theatre was open, Joe was around ten years old. He says that there were always long lines to the theatre on Saturday nights. Before the movie started, kids would watch adults smoking cigarettes while they waited in line. When an

adult discarded a cigarette butt, the kids flocked to it like seagulls. And if one kid stumbled across a butt of a cigar, that was the ultimate prize, winning the approval of all their friends.

Now the Russel building holds The Boro Girl Boutique, owned by Crystal Foy. The aged hardwood floors creek under your feet and the ceilings hang low. The outside bricks of the store are ones brought over from the Tarrymore Hotel after it was razed. The Boro Girl Boutique is one of the most frequented businesses in downtown Swansboro.

Captain Joe can often be seen across the street sitting on the exterior bench of Front Street Grocery, the same building his dad built in 1950. I find him there more

*Captain Joe Webb at Front Street Grocery*

than three times a week, sparking up conversations with anyone that passes by or feeding those Muscovy ducks. I told you earlier about the men of yesteryear always hanging out on the docks and Front Street. This is Joe's version of continuing that tradition.

On the right side of Yana's and Front Street Grocery is vacant land with a fence around it. You can't tell that there was a building once on it. That piece of property held Carl's Café and Fred Bell's Soda Shop before it turned into one of Swansboro's most notorious bars called the Jolly Roger. The infamous watering hole was opened up by Carl Tolson and stuck around for decades. From Captain Joe and other locals, I'm told the bar had pool tables. Money was often wagered at those same tables. Upstairs, men placed money on games of Hearts or different variations of poker. Just like Codfish, Jolly Roger had some wild, crazy, and unforgettable times.

Chief of Police, M.T. Maness was dispatched to the Jolly Roger a time or two to break up fights or to take a drunk home during Jolly Roger's era. The building itself was eventually moved by Tolson's daughter named Zeta to Bear Creek, some eight miles away. While writing this book, I would meet Carl Tolson's granddaughter named Gloria Sanders, a woman with a zany personality. She added stories about her grandad. Carl Tolson ran a freight boat called the Charmer in the 1930s and 1940s, carrying goods and supplies to Swansboro. He was also the first person in town with a truck. Just like he did with the Charmer, he used that truck to bring in goods and supplies to Swansboro.

Further down Front Street, you will find the Willy Nilly Warehouse on top of Bake, Bottle, and Brew. Willy Nilly is a unique gift shop that offers quirky gifts, coastal décor, jewelry, and classic games, as well as an ice-cream parlor and coffee bar. Bake, Bottle, and Brew offers wine and beer. It also has an outdoor area where live bands typically play five days a week. The building itself is fairly new. That same land once held the Littleton fish and crab houses.

Other places of note on Front Street are local gift shops like Merrow, Silver Line, and Starlings. Last but not least is Mercantile, which is where the former fish house run by Jim Canaday was located. Further down on Church Street, you can find other businesses such as Through the Looking Glass, George's Cigar Shop, and Church Street Deli owned by Josh Sawyer. Even though the above are current day businesses, tomorrow they will be part of Swansboro's history.

One Thursday morning I met with the ladies of Swansboro's Historical Society, while there, Captain Joe phoned me and said someone wanted to meet me. Being only two minutes away, I rushed to his house on Main Street. Inside, the captain sat in his recliner and an older lady with beautiful piercing eyes stood near him. I introduced myself to her and met Miss Diane-Redd Williams. She had heard about the book and wanted to contribute. First, Diane told me she was the widow of R.L. Williams Jr., the friend that gave Joe the beer mug from the Codfish bar. I loved connecting the dots. Didn't expect more than that but welcomed her ties to Joe and Swansboro.

As we talked the information would get much, much better. Miss Diane added that Mabel Gerock was her aunt. I had heard Mabel's name at least a dozen times in the previous two months. The only notable mention was her being the owner and operator of the one-time Swan Café. Then Diane asked, "Did you know my aunt once owned the Tarrymore Hotel?"

I didn't know this. Miss Diane had my full attention. My mind went into overload when she admitted, "I still have the original keys to the hotel at my house."

This couldn't get any better. Right in front of me was R.L.

*Mabel Gerock, photo courtesy of Diane Williams*

Williams Jr.'s widow and niece of Mabel Gerock, a name that kept coming up but seemed to be a mystery. She had keys to the Tarrymore Hotel that had been razed nearly sixty years ago! Immediately, we made plans for me to stop by her house that same week. I took Miss Diane's phone number and gave her the biggest of hugs. I was super excited, knowing she held on to a piece of history at her home, in her mind, and in her heart. I could not wait to see Miss Diane at her home off Swansboro-Belgrade Road. I couldn't wait to see those keys and to hear the stories from Miss Diane Redd-Williams.

When that day came, I ended up arriving an hour early because I was so anxious. After entering the modest house, I was offered crackers with exotic toppings. While eating, Miss Diane retold stories about her dear R.L. and her Aunt Mabel. While listening for a few minutes, I noticed a hanging key to the Tarrymore Hotel. The key had probably been there for decades, no one knowing what it belonged to. But you and I do. I included photos of me holding this treasure. This key could be over 100 years old. This was one of the biggest finds yet.

On the table in her dining room, old newspapers, and old photographs were spread out. Slowly and carefully, I went through the items, not wanting to damage them. Most of the

pictures were of R.L William's Jr. childhood and his side of the family. Digging deeper, my heart nearly stopped when an old photo of Aunt Mabel Redd-Gerock stared at me. I held the photograph in my hands and asked Miss Diane to give me all the history she could about this mysterious woman.

*Photo courtesy of Diane Williams,*
*Tarrymore Hotel key*

Mabel's father once owned one of the largest rock quarries on the East Coast, a few miles outside Swansboro. Days before selling off his company called Superior Stone Company in 1941, he passed away. His family would miss out on a large sum of money due to pending contracts her father had with the purchasing company. Still, Mabel and her eleven siblings inherited a tidy amount but not nearly what it would have been if her father had lived longer. Today, that same rock quarry is known as Martin Marietta.

Even though Mabel received money after her father's death, she can be described as an independent, hardworking, and ambitious woman. Instead of living on the inheritance, she put the money to work for her. Keep in mind, women of this era didn't own many businesses. But this did not describe Mabel. She would first purchase a building at the corner of Moore and Front Street and open the Swan Café. Miss Diane informed me that her Aunt Mabel could cook anything. One of her original recipes was that of hushpuppies. It's said that a man named Walter Thompson borrowed her little recipe from her and patented it. Could be true or could be a family tale that was passed down. But either way, Walter Thompson did patent 'Thompson's Fireside Hush Puppy Mix,' which bore a Swansboro address on the product's bag.

Many of Swan Café's customers were travelers that stayed at the Tarrymore Hotel, directly next door. The restaurant's success was largely due to Mabel's personality and how she treated customers. She was also known by her family and customers to be very entertaining.

Sometime later, Mabel would go on to purchase the Tarrymore Hotel when it went up for sale. Already rare in that day of age for a woman to own one business, Mabel now owned the restaurant and hotel. She didn't stop there. Her boyfriend at the time was Captain Joe's idol in Vincent Ward. Vincent was one of the better fishermen in the area, but he didn't have much money. This is where Mabel came into the picture. As a proprietor and investor, she bought a fishing vessel and named the boat 'Jean Ann', after her daughter. Think back to those days, men typically named boats after the wife or daughter. Mabel joined an exclusive men's club, revolutionizing the industry. She would be a trailblazer. Vincent would be the captain of the Jean Ann for her.

Vincent Ward was sort of a pioneer himself.

*Captain Jesse Moore, Captain Vince Ward, Captain Charlie Buckmaster, Sr. and Captain Little Jesse Moore*

Local fishermen looked up to him and asked for advice. I added a photo that Captain Joe has at his home. In the picture, you can see Captain Jesse Moore, Captain Vincent Ward, Captain Charlie Buckmaster Sr., and 'Little Jesse' Moore. Vincent appears to be demonstrating a technique to the other veteran fishermen with Swansboro in the background.

Before Jean Ann began chartering customers, Mabel footed the bill for Vincent and other fishermen to travel to Florida. A popular species of fish at the time were King Mackerel. Even though they moved through the waters near Swansboro, the local fishermen didn't know much else about them. They were sent to Florida to learn more about the fish and to catch King Mackerel.

After their return, Mabel had a big hand in Vincent's success as a charter boat captain. The Jean Ann was one of the most sought out boats at that time. Some drama did come Mabel's way. I was told that it was frowned upon for women to live with men if they weren't married during that era. And Mabel allowed Vincent to live with her. After a year or two, Mabel allegedly was run out of Onslow County for the supposed scandal. As an independent and strong woman, she built her own house in nearby by Cedar Point, three miles on the opposite side of Swansboro and Onslow County. Vincent would live with her there too.

Miss Diane shared a funny story. She and her siblings called Vincent, 'Uncle Den Den.' They all loved the man. I was told he was kind, generous and always made them laugh. However, when they visited her Aunt Mabel's house in Cedar

Point, she made it look like Uncle Den Den lived in a small building behind her home. But Miss Diane and her family knew better. Even though the two were not married, it became obvious that Vincent and Mabel stayed in the same house.

Miss Mabel lived a colorful life, so I just knew I had to write about some of her contributions to Swansboro since other history books nearly erased her from the past. Her story should not be forgotten. If she were living in today's world, Mabel would be in business magazines and have newspaper articles written about her. I was so thankful to learn more about Mabel through her niece in Miss Diane.

Before leaving Miss Diane, I thanked her immensely and promised to come back in a week or two. She said to me, "Thank you for telling everyone about Captain Joe whom we know and love, even when he can be a pain in our ass sometimes. Take care and continue doing what you were meant to do. You have a very inspiring story and hopefully, you will open other's eyes and hearts. I feel that God had a plan for you and you are being obedient."

We hugged. I found another friend while working on this book. I got to hear wonderful stories from a woman that called Swansboro home. I learned so much from her in those two hours we spoke. Right before I left, Miss Diane said I could have most of those items and pictures she possessed after she died, including the Tarrymore Hotel keys. If this does happen, it will all be given to the Swansboro Historical Society where it belongs. What a sweet, sweet encounter.

I'm handed a handwritten letter on my way out the door.

In it, the letter, Diane Redd-Williams writes:

*'In September 2021, I lost my soulmate and love of my life in R.L. Williams Jr. Joe and R.L. were lifetime friends. They grew up playing and running the streets of Swansboro. They also ran charters side by side with Billy Anna and R.L.'s boat, the Ranger II. They partied together and always had each other's back. R.L. and Joe loved each other, and I was fortunate to be a part of that union for over 30 years.'*

*'There was no need for entertainment when those two were together. Joe and R.L. talked on the phone frequently and Joe said R.L. was his therapist. In later years, R.L. battled Parkinson's disease. They took day trips together to Harker's Island to visit their old fishing buddies and boat builders. They would come back with smiles and laughs and many stories.'*

*'Since R.L.'s death, Joe and I check on one another with a phone call or visit. I cherish our talks and the little bit of R.L. that Joe shares with me. Some make me laugh. Some make me shed tears. Joe Webb loves people (esp. women). He loves fishing but most of all, he loves his little hometown of Swansboro, North Carolina.'*

- Diane Williams

Two weeks later, Melissa Webb, the girl I had gone to high school with, and Joe's third cousin had some fascinating news for me that she had discovered. She rented office space in the same house that Mabel Gerock owned in Cedar Point, the same one she lived in with Vincent Ward.

*Port hole off the Jean Ann*

Melissa Webb uncovered one of the portholes from the boat Jean Ann. Everything started tying together. History began piecing itself together with the good people of Swansboro sharing their stories and lives with me.

*Steering helm to Ranger boat, Chad Hollamon photo courtesy of Diane Williams*

*A young local proud of his catch with Jean Ann beside him. Photo courtesy of Diane Williams*

# CHAPTER TWELVE
# A NIGHT WITH DR. J.P. CORBETT AND DR. WILLIAM SHARPE

When nighttime approaches, the quaint village of Swansboro begins to shut down. Town ordinances are in place on local businesses for a particular reason. The powers of the city council didn't want Swansboro to be a party place, full of drunks and bad behavior, similar to the days when the bars Codfish and Jolly Roger were at their peak. Downtown Swansboro doesn't even have establishments that serve exclusively alcohol. Food must be offered at these same places that do sell liquor and beer. Subsequently, after 10:00 PM, you will hardly see a soul on the streets. Almost reminds me of a ghost town.

Sporadically, I like to roam the downtown area during this time. With no people or cars around, it places me in an earlier decade or century. Gives me the feel of what Swansboro was like many years ago. The only noises you hear are the wind howling and the ocean current splashing against the docks. Even the ducks seem to be sleeping during this time, leaving me with complete solitude and seclusion.

On one such recent late wintertime stroll, I glanced through the glass front stores as I aimlessly wandered the sidewalks, glimpsing reflections of myself. I zig-zagged Front Street at my leisure or sometimes just stayed in the middle of the road as I didn't have to worry about cars coming and going. My pace slowed considerably when approaching the historical homes that had been present for centuries.

Don't know why but that night, I studied the chimneys of each house as I ambled through Elm and Walnut Streets. Before electricity was common for those houses, I could envision the only lights coming from the house emitted through candles and lit fires coming from the fireplace. I imagined smoke rising from the chimneys, those same fires used to keep families warm in the wintertime.

I recalled an old story given to me about one of the town's past well-known doctors in J.P. Corbett. Doctor Corbett was the only Swansboro medical practitioner from 1930 to 1962. Being the only doctor around, he had to make house calls no matter the time of day. On one such call in the early morning hours, he walked the same streets as I did. On the way to his destination to deliver a baby, he noticed flames from the window of a house. He ran to the house, banged on the door, and woke up its occupants. With the help of Dr. Corbett, the fire was eventually put out, only causing minimal damage. He stayed for a while to make sure everyone was okay. I could only imagine what would have happened if he wasn't walking by at that ungodly hour. Dr. Corbett left the family and continued to another house down the street where he eventually delivered a baby. That night, Dr. Corbett saved lives and birthed a new life.

Captain Joe Webb repeated another story I had heard several times about Dr. Corbett. In the old Swansboro High School, which is now the middle school, there's a bronze plaque hanging up that dedicates the gymnasium to Dr. Corbett. There was a ceremony held when the plaque was unveiled. The bleachers were full of students and town folks. During the ceremony, the person presenting the plaque to Dr. Corbett asked everyone in the crowd to raise their hands if they were delivered by him. It's said that nearly everyone in that gym had their hands up. Captain Joe, Jack Dudley, Norman Wells, Bobby Wells, Mr. Rhue, and hundreds of other locals were all delivered by J.P. Corbett.

Dr. Corbett wasn't a native of Swansboro. He moved his family here in 1930 from Red Oak, North Carolina, after receiving degrees from the University of North Carolina and Washington University in St. Louis. Washington University was a prestigious college at that time. Dr. Corbett was even a member of the national academic medical honor society Alpha Omega Alpha in medical school.

Keep in mind, this was the era immediately after Wall Street crashed and during the Great Depression. Jobs were almost non-existent at this time. Of all the places in the United States he could choose to practice medicine, Dr. Corbett opted for the sparsely settled coastal region and somewhat poverty-stricken Swansboro, full of farmers and fishermen. His first office would be a dusty room above the post office on the north side of Main Street in a building near the waterfront.

Also, keep in mind, this was before any bridge had been built across the White Oak River. To reach many of his clients in Cedar Point in Carteret County or any of the nearby islands, he had to take a boat. And sometimes he had to travel in the middle of the night. There are many stories about how he often got paid. Since so many people didn't have money in those days, he was often compensated with hams, vegetables, and fish. After one such delivery of a newborn, the family gave him a Bogue Sound watermelon. Dr. Corbett never complained about it. He was called to serve where needed, and not necessarily where there was money or wealth.

Being the only doctor available to the hundreds of Swansboro citizens, I was told Dr. Corbett worked all the time with no days off. Even when he was enjoying family time at his house, people would come knocking on his door with a new emergency. I've read that people frequently came to his house in the middle of the night in dire need of his services. Still, Dr. Corbett never complained. He helped others out, no matter what time of day or night it was.

Not only did Dr. Corbett attend to the locals, but he also served as a physician to the Swansboro Coast Guard Station during World War II and was president of the Onslow County Medical Society. To the locals of Swansboro, he was trusted because his 'accuracy of diagnoses and the efficacy of his cures have become almost a legend in his day and has produced in his patients a confidence in anything the doctor prescribes.'

I had the honor of meeting Dr. Corbett's grandson, Jim while working on this book. He, his wife, and two daughters happened to be visiting from Connecticut that particular week. We exchanged phone numbers and stayed in touch over the ensuing months. Jim answered questions I had about his granddad, and he would share stories he'd heard about Captain Joe Webb as a bonus.

Dr. Corbett's house in Swansboro still stands but is unoccupied at the moment. It's heartbreaking

*Photo courtesy of Jim Corbett*

because of the history it holds and because the property has one of the better views of the White Oak River, sitting tall on a high bluff. I drive by the old house occasionally and sit there envisioning what life was like for the doctor and his family more than a half-century ago.

Dr. Corbett's descendants continue to have a strong presence in the area, with his daughter Patsy living on a nearby property. The bronze plaque in the middle school gymnasium remains. And there is also a section of Highway 24 dedicated to Dr. Corbett. I find satisfaction in the fact that the town rightfully honored this man. Not only did he deliver hundreds of babies, but he would also serve them as young children, teenagers, and in their adulthood. There couldn't be a bigger impact from one individual the way Dr. Corbett had for Swansboro.

There is another doctor that contributed to Swansboro's rich history. And he was actually present around the time of Dr. Corbett, but he didn't practice medicine in the state of North Carolina. Dr. William Sharpe, a neurosurgeon from New York originally came to North Carolina in 1914 to hunt  ducks. He especially enjoyed hunting on Bear Island where it wasn't too cold in the winter and wasn't too hot in the summer months.

Dr. Sharpe hired a black man named John Lewis Hurst to tend to his boat and as a hunting guide when he came to Swansboro. As time went on, Dr. Sharpe became so impressed with John's knowledge of the outdoors, he hired him full-time. In 1920, Dr. Sharpe was in search of a perfect retreat from New York. He asked John, "Find me land in an area that is beautiful, isolated, and has an abundance of fish and game."

Three years later, Dr. Sharpe purchased 'The Hammocks', 878 acres of various islands and wetlands just outside Swansboro. John found the perfect retreat for Dr. Sharpe and his family. The doctor loved the beauty and the seclusion of the island that offered duck, quail, turkey, and goose hunting. The land was also good for growing tobacco, cotton, corn, peanuts, watermelons, and other garden crops. The waters around it were filled with bass, bluefish, flounder, clams, oysters, and shrimp.

Dr. Sharpe's land was occupied with a two-story house, a cotton gin, and other buildings around the property. When the Sharpe family came down to visit, they took a train from New York to Wilson, North Carolina. From there, John Hurst picked them up in an automobile. John's wife, part Native American named Gertrude was hired as a cook and housekeeper. During the 1920s, the Sharpe and Hurst families mingled together on the Hammocks.

I do want to share a story about the Hammocks during the late 1920s when prohibition was in full effect. History suggests that bootleggers and smugglers often used the Hammocks and nearby islands to hide their alcohol as they clandestinely ran up and down the coast. Dr. Sharpe complained to the authorities about the illicit traffic, but the authorities did nothing about it. Another legend is that two shady characters approached Dr. Sharpe at his office in New York one day and offered to buy the island from him. He politely declined their offer but added that it would be nice if they left a little something behind if they used his island. By the end of prohibition, Dr. Sharpe had an endless supply of whisky and other liquors hidden around the island.

Dr. Corbett and Dr. Sharpe met each other around 1930. This would end up being a decades-long friendship. Dr. Sharpe invited Dr. Corbett and his family over to the Hammocks during the summer months. They discussed medicine, hunting, and fishing while their children grew up together. From Dr. Corbett's grandson, I learned the two doctors even wrote letters to each other between New York and North Carolina.

*Photos courtesy of Dr. Corbett's grandson, Jim Corbett*

I did find another neat story about the estate at the Hammocks. In 1937, the state of North Carolina made plans to construct a road that would run from Swansboro to Wilmington, North Carolina, coming extremely close to the Hammocks. The state deemed it would make the area 'more valuable.' Dr. Sharpe sought relief to stop the road from being built. The state denied him any relief and continued with their plans to build the road. That's when the doctor turned to a higher power.

While Dr. Sharpe was on a train from Wilson, North Carolina to New York, he decided to stop in Washington D.C. The President of the United States at the time was Franklin Roosevelt, a Harvard classmate of Dr. Sharpe's. He arrived at the White House and requested a sit down with the president. The meeting lasted three minutes. Within a day, plans for the intended road ceased, saving the Hammocks from having extra visitors. The state eventually went with paving a road in Queen's Creek, some three miles away from the Hammocks.

When Dr. Sharpe wrote his will later in life, he opted to leave the entire Hammock's estate to John Hurst, his friend, and caretaker of nearly forty years. Some residents questioned the decision by the doctor to leave the Hammocks in charge of a black man. Dr. Sharpe and John Hurst were also threatened through intimidation. The doctor refused to back down. He placed ads in the local newspaper offering a reward of $5,000 for the arrest and conviction of anyone damaging the Hammocks or injuring its personnel. Nothing bad ever happened.

I found a quote that will explain the doctor's true feelings about his longtime caretaker. Dr. William Sharpe said about John Hurst, 'Looking back over those thirty-eight years, I realize I gained from him more common-sense, useful bits of knowledge than from any other man I have ever known. Not only because he is a master at farming, stock-raising, and outdoor life, but because he is a great philosopher.'

It's said John Hurst decided that tending to the estate was too much work, so he suggested to Dr. Sharpe to turn it over to the North Carolina Black Teachers Association instead. That was exactly what happened after Dr. Sharpe died in 1960. The estate was given to the organization for educational and recreational purposes. It would stay a black-only recreational island until the civil rights act of 1964 passed.

Today, the Hammock's is now called Hammock's Beach. Thousands of people come here every year by ferry or personal boat. This unspoiled island is full of wildlife and the water is full of fish. The house of Dr. Sharpe's retreat no longer stands but the indelible mark the doctor left behind remains present.

*USO Building*

# CHAPTER THIRTEEN
# ADDITIONAL IMPORTANT LANDMARKS
# U.S.O. BUILDING

Earlier I touched on the arrival of the military in the 1940s. You read about the influx of tens of thousands of new residents coming to the greater Onslow County area. New forms of entertainment were established during this time. As a result, the U.S.O. (United States Organization) was formed. Its mission was to provide recreation for on-leave members of the U.S. armed forces and their families.

In a matter of months in 1941, the U.S.O built four community centers in Jacksonville for those that served. The U.S.O. gave service personnel a home away from home. Dances were held at all four locations, providing the young locals with the opportunity to become acquainted with the troops. As a result, friendships were formed. Romantic relationships were spawned, and marriages were created.

When it came time for the military to build a U.S.O. community center in Swansboro, funding came up short. Dr. Sharpe came in to give a helping hand. The purchase price was $10,000 and Dr. Sharpe footed half the bill for the U.S.O to be built in downtown Swansboro. The land chosen for the intended building would be the same location as where Captain Otway Burn's statue stands today. I have included a photo of the white building so you will know what the area looked like from 1942 until the statue was erected in 1983.

The U.S.O. was an instant success for the community of Swansboro. Dinners, dances, and parties were held nearly every night during World War II. There were non-stop celebrations after the war to honor our brave soldiers. They say it was a beautiful time for Swansboro. It wasn't just the young locals and young Marines attending these functions. In Jack Dudley's book, you can see photos of kids playing in the foreground while older citizens sit at tables in the back.

When I first heard or read about the U.S.O. in Swansboro, I wondered how it worked with the young local men. I do have a personal story that's kind of hard to admit. Earlier in the book I told you that I was hell on wheels in the mid-1990s when I was 18 or 19 years old. I'd often get drunk and regularly get into fights. Some of those fights were with Marines. Sometimes we fought just for the sake of fighting, too much testosterone I guess from both sides. But then I'd challenge a handful when they were talking to the local girls. In my immature mind, they were taking our girls – as stupid as it sounds now.

So, I asked people like Captain Joe and Ann Shuller how young local men reacted to the Marines back during the times of the U.S.O. All were in agreement that relations were more than cordial. I was reminded that times were different, having come off a war. These soldiers fought for our freedom and were welcomed as heroes. I didn't grow up in a time of war but now that I'm older, I see things much differently. I will add this; even though I got into numerous fights with Marines during this time I did make some lifelong friends with a few of them when I was young. They ended up staying in the area after serving in the military and we've maintained contact since.

I've touched on how intertwined the older families were in Swansboro, with some women having multiple common last names. With the incoming military of the 1940s and 1950s, the dating pool would be much larger, which was a good thing. Some of the local Swansboro women would go on to marry some of the same Marines that served in the area. The community grew much stronger because of the military's presence, by adding to the workforce and filling a void where it was needed.

The old white U.S.O. building was eventually torn down, ending another era in Swansboro's history, but I couldn't omit the importance of it. There is a small monument near the Captain Otway Burns statue, rightfully honoring our military. Now when I drive by the statute, I just don't think of Otway. I think of the hundreds of people congregating under the roof of the once-standing U.S.O., dancing, eating, and celebrating. It brought people together during a tense time for our country.

While I touched on a little about the U.S.O. building and its importance, I would like to mention a few more landmarks a little outside of the Swansboro historic district. Each has its

CLYDE PHILIP'S SEAFOOD MARKET

historical significance. Between the two bridges leading out of Swansboro, there is a small island where a few businesses stand. One is that of Clyde Philip's Seafood Market. You can't miss the old shrimp boats docked behind their pink building. Since 1954, Clyde's has been an icon on the coast.

It's another gathering place for men, where they sit in chairs in the morning, and drink coffee. When I pass by there I often see a handful of trucks parked in the steep gravel driveway. Not only has the business withstood hurricanes, flooding, and other challenges, it has outlasted over a dozen other fish houses that were at home in the area.

Jimmy Phillips, an eighty-year-old Swansboro local, took over the business after the death of his father, Clyde in 1980. Recently, I visited the Tideland News office. There, Editor-in-chief Jimmy Williams allowed me to dig through old newspapers. I came across an article that was around forty years old. The article detailed the end of Clyde's life. Before he died, Clyde had one request, he wanted to be driven to his seafood house to see it one more time. On March 14, 1980, in the middle of a snowstorm, his son Jimmy and other family members took Clyde to his beloved seafood market in the back of the ambulance. The ambulance they were in backed up to the establishment. Since Clyde couldn't walk, he asked for the rear doors to be opened up. Once they were open, Clyde sat there looking at the business he started years ago. After a good thirty minutes he said something along the lines of, 'Okay, I can go home now.' The doors were shut and Clyde returned home. He died two weeks later.

I had the honor of meeting Jimmy and his son Clyde while writing this book. As I sat there a steady flow of customers came in to purchase all sorts of seafood. I could tell that Jimmy and his

son loved what they did. They knew most of the customers' first names that came in and what they liked. Their old-school mentality was like Captain

*RIVIERA CLUB*

Joe's and others that I've met along the way.

Before leaving I promised myself, I would return, maybe even for a cup of morning coffee. Clyde's Phillip's Seafood is a must-stop for those visiting Swansboro.

Just past the two Swansboro bridges, you will enter Cedar Point. Once there you will see an odd-shaped building on the opposite side of Dudley's Marina across Highway 24. That same building was known as the Riviera Restaurant, established in 1949 by Charlie Buckmaster Sr. and his two sons Joe and Charlie Jr. In the first three years of being open, their seafood restaurant thrived. It went so well that Charlie Sr. left operations to Joe and Charlie Jr. so he could be a full-time charter captain on his boat the Douglas, named after his grandson.

At that time, the U.S.O building was used for reasons other than weekly entertainment. Joe and Charlie Jr. saw a niche and wanted to create an environment of a nightclub, full of music and dancing. They renamed the Riviera Restaurant the Riviera Club. The sons placed a huge neon sign on top of the building that read, 'Riviera Club.' A large palm tree rested beside the sign. The biggest modification was the construction of another grand room on the right side of the restaurant, basically doubling its size. There, a large dance floor was laid down with a stage for live bands.

This was the place to go for young adults during that era. Local bands played on the weekend while dances were held during the week. The Riviera Club was a place to let loose, the latest dances were on display. I'm told that the club stayed booked and would be packed every weekend. The end of the era came to a screeching halt with the sudden death of Charlie Jr. While I visited the Tideland News, I came across another article, detailing the events that surrounded Charlie Jr.'s death. After an apparent self-inflicted gunshot wound, Charlie Jr. was rushed to the hospital in an ambulance. Charlie Sr. rode in the back with him where Charlie Jr. lay dying in his father's arms. Today, when I pass by that odd-shaped building I think of the Buckmaster family and what they endured. No father should watch their children die and especially in the manner of Charlie Buckmaster. Captain Charlie Buckmaster Sr. was another legend for Swansboro.

*COAST GUARD STATION*

Earlier in the book I wrote about the Coast Guard Station overlooking Bogue Inlet in Emerald Isle in the 1900s. From 1905-1912, the original structure was called Bogue Inlet Lifesaving

Station. I found out through old newspapers that during that time, the lifesavers had been charged to row as far as five miles into the Atlantic Ocean and had saved as many as 75 people. They saved passengers from various troubled ships. Hard to keep in mind that they didn't have motors yet.

During the active season, the lifesavers had to watch over the horizon, both day and night. Other duties consisted of patrolling the beach to see flares, signal flags, or other hints of distress. Their boats were called, 'surfboats.' Six men were responsible for the 3,000-pound boat. They had to launch it down a ramp into Bogue Sound. One man steered the tiller, while five men had to row.

In 1914, they changed the name to U.S. Coast Guard Station. Then, in 1939, a new building was put up beside the existing one. They would use the old Bogue Inlet Lifesaving Station for storage and other random uses. In 1950, the government decided to sell off the old structure. The government asked for the public to submit closed bids.

Only one bid was submitted for $25.00 and that was from George Merritt Jr., a distant relative of my friend Billy Parkin. Being the sole bidder, he rightfully owned it on the condition he had to move it. George used a barge and another boat to relocate the old station three miles to Cedar Point. Once George Merrit Sr. got it there, he turned it into a private club called, 'American Legion Hut.' A few years later he turned it into a nightclub, full of dancing, dining, and gambling.

Today, the building remains standing in the same location in Cedar Point, only about one mile from the Swansboro bridges.

*OCTAGON HOUSE*

Another unique house in Cedar Point is the Octagon House, named after its eight sides. I've included two photos of it, one old and one new. You can see the transformation it underwent, especially with the wrap-around porch. By personal account, it didn't always look that way. Back in the 1990s, my friends and I use to hang out at the house. It was dilapidated and nearly abandoned inside a large cow pasture. My friends and I played Hide n Seek there while on copious amounts of hallucinogenic drugs. Told you I was a knucklehead. Anyhow, we chased each other throughout the house and around the large property. Little did I know I would be writing about the Octagon House thirty years later.

The original two-story house was built in 1855 by Edward Hill. Both floors have nearly the identical floorplan. Two squared rooms and four with a rectangular shape. There are four chimneys, meaning each room had a fireplace. Edward Hill built the house in that octagon shape because he disliked the howling of the wind. His idea was that by building a house in that kind of a round shape, the wind would not strike as hard as if was exposed. Some also believe the house can withstand hurricane-strength winds. It has lasted through at least two dozen major hurricanes, including Hurricane Hazel, so I can see the validity in that belief.

I did some research on what the house was made of to make it so durable. For one, cedar wood was used, off of the Hill plantation. It is resistant to corrosion by salt air. The nails were made of copper and dipped in oil to make them nearly water-resistant. Some of the newer houses in the area are not as sturdy as the Octagon House.

There is an old family graveyard on the property that made it even more eerie when my friends

and I played Hide n Seek. The last names of Hill and Jones are etched on most of the headstones. The reason why Jones is one of the common last names is that Edward's daughter named Mary inherited the property and she went on to marry Robert H. Jones. The couple had eight children, and all were raised in the Octagon house.

Today, the Octagon House and nearby area is a sprawling property. Public nature trails surround the house, allowing the average person to admire its beauty. I've been out there a time or two this past year, this time not on drugs. The cow pasture is no longer there, and the graveyard is fenced in. Deer and other wildlife can typically be seen roaming between the trees. The family that restored it has done a magnificent job with the home.

*W.T. Casper and Chad Hollamon*

# CHAPTER FOURTEEN
## W.T. CASPER

I finally got the opportunity to meet another legend of Swansboro, W.T. Casper. Truthfully, if I would have written this book a year or two earlier, I could have done it with both Captain Joe Webb and W.T. Casper. Joe and W.T. are the same age and have been lifelong friends. Sadly, W.T.'s health has been steadily declining in recent years. His memory is not what it used to be, but his presence remains large with the locals and those that visit here.

*Captain Joe Webb center, W.T. Casper to his left and other Swansboro locals, photo courtesy of Susan Casper.*

When I first met W.T. in the 1990's he was larger than life. Not only did he own and operate one of the biggest marinas in the area, but he also built boats and could fix anything that had a motor. He was a man's man. Every man wanted to be like him and if they couldn't, they at least wanted to be around this local celebrity. W.T. Casper and his family have contributed to the improvement of Swansboro for at least four generations.

I was initially a little nervous about meeting W.T., I didn't know what I was going to ask him. I just knew I wanted to dedicate this chapter to him. After stepping foot inside his huge and well kempt marina that held hundreds of boats, I met Susan Casper, W.T.'s wife. She is also the same age as Joe and her husband. Having grown up in Swansboro too, Susan had story after story of Captain Joe Webb and other bits of historical facts about her hometown. I sincerely enjoyed speaking to her. She's just as sharp as anyone half her age, and her intellect and sense of humor are unmatched.

She showed me hundreds of photos in scrapbooks she had saved, most of them having to do with damage hurricanes had left behind over the past thirty years or so. The others were of Casper's Marina and the changes it has undergone since the Casper's acquired the property back in the 1940s. W.T.'s grandad Joe Casper bought the land from Swansboro Land and Lumber Company and built the marina with W.T.'s father, Bill, in 1945.

After talking to Susan for about thirty minutes, W.T. walked in. Susan introduced us and she left him and me alone. I was nearly star-struck. When my words finally came out I said, "I'm writing a book about Captain Joe Webb along with some history of Swansboro."

W.T. answered, "Captain I."

I assumed him to be confused with my intentions about the book but I would soon find out the man still had a sense of humor. I corrected him, "Captain Joe Webb."

He gave me a hint of a smile and answered, "Captain Joe is Captain I." He paused before continuing, "Captain I know this, and Captain I know that. That's Captain Joe for you. That's my nickname for him." he said.

I burst out laughing at his joke. But saying that, my mom always told me there is always a little bit of truth in a little bit of playing. W.T.'s health might be declining but he knew Captain Joe better than anyone around Swansboro. The two have been friends for nearly 80 years! That's some history right there. W.T. had been here his whole life except for the four years he attended East Carolina University in Greenville, North Carolina.

I sat there with W.T. for close to an hour, asking him questions about the marina and various stories I had heard. After the death of his father Bill, W.T. took over the marina. Imagine being thirty years old and all of a sudden, being responsible for such a large enterprise. W.T. took off and ran with it. Not only did he enlarge and modernize the marina, but he would also go on to build over a hundred skiffs with the Casper name on it. His family's legacy is a testament to W.T. and Susan's hard work and efforts.

W.T. also had a hand in helping to construct Joe's boat, the Billy Anna II. When the hull was shipped to Swansboro, W.T., and Joe spent months putting in the diesel engines and retrofitting her with components used for fishing and navigation. I could only imagine the two legends working side by side. I left W.T. that afternoon, thankful for the conversations I had with this man. I rushed to find Captain Joe to ask him questions about his old friend.

I wandered Water, Main, and Front Streets, in search of Joe until I found him at Yana's Restaurant along with two other men. I sat at a table beside them as they exchanged stories. One man brought up the time former North Carolina Governor Hunt visited Swansboro some thirty or forty years prior. I intently listened in on the story. While the governor ate at The Snap Dragon Restaurant, a young Captain Joe came charging in and blew past his security detail.

Captain Joe put the governor in sort of a headlock and asked him, "Why, aren't you the guvna?"

The governor waved off his security detail as he didn't think the captain was a threat. He answered Joe, "Yes sir. I am the governor. How can I help you?"

Captain Joe said, "I'm going to take you and your men fishing and you ain't gotta pay me a red cent."

At the end of the story, I laughed along with

the other men. Just another day with the captain where people shared stories with Joe and about him. For the next twenty minutes, I sat there in silence, waiting for some one-on-one time with Joe. I wanted to ask him questions about W.T. But I didn't want to do it with other people around. Pretty soon, the other men left, and I was alone with the captain. I switched tables and sat across from him.

Small talk commenced. I asked, "How are you doing? You go to the doctor this morning?"

He gave me a stern look and answered, "Got to have my heart checked out next week. Not too thrilled about that."

"I can drive you if you want. Where's the appointment?" I said.

"Morehead City. That's alright. My sister's taking me." Joe replied.

We sat there for a minute or two without saying a word. I detected an uneasiness about the upcoming doctor visit. Joe of all people knew how fragile life can be. It can be gone in the flash of a second. I wondered what went through Joe's mind. Did he question would it be his last year of living? Did he visit the ones in the hospital, questioning if it would be the last time he would see that person? Did he eat at Yana's imagining it being one of the last times he would dine there? Did he look at the Billy Anna and ask when would be her final journey with him as the captain? He disliked doctors, and having to go get a check-up on his heart probably scared the living crap out of him. I'm sure he would trade to be anywhere in the world rather than be in that doctor's office, hooked up to all kinds of machines.

I changed the subject, "I'm ready to go out on the Billy Anna when you are." I said.

"Won't be long now. Should be fixed soon enough." Joe said.

"Good, 'cause I'm good and ready for a little salt therapy. Been over twenty years since I've been out on her. After hearing all these experiences on the Billy Anna, I'm ready for my own." I said. After a few seconds passed by I added, "I saw W.T. today.'

He smiled and remarked, "Oh, yeah. How's he doing? I need to make it that way to see him and Susan sometime." Joe added.

"I met her today too. I didn't know she was a Jones before marrying W.T. She was the librarian at Swansboro High School when I went to school there." I told him.

"Her mom Elsie was a teacher as well. W.T. tried his hand at teaching for one year after college. Think he taught Industrial Arts or something like that." Joe told me.

I asked, "Did he help you build the Billy Anna?"

"After the hull was shipped here, we kept it at Casper's Marina until it was complete. W.T. knows everything there is about a boat. He got me up and running after a few weeks. Did you ever notice the compass on the Billy Anna?" Joe asked.

"No sir," I said.

"W.T. gave me that. The compass came off one of Ernest Hemingway's boats." Joe said.

"You got to be freaking kidding me," I incredulously commented back.

I could tell Captain Joe loved this story. He added, "Yep. A few years back, W.T. gave me that as a gift. It's one of my prized possessions."

"You got some good friends. The man gave you an object from Ernest Hemingway's boat. How cool is that?" I said.

# CHAPTER FIFTEEN
## THE BILLY ANNA II RIDES AGAIN
### JUNE 19, 2023

Today was one of those magical days. The sun beamed down with just a few wispy clouds overhead. A light southwesterly breeze assisted in making the hot temperature tolerable. The seas were calm, giving the ocean surface the appearance of glass across the water. Although tourists are already here in droves, it's not bumper-to-bumper traffic like it will be on the upcoming Fourth of July weekend. For the people that live here year-round, days like today are why they love this beautiful area so much.

Sometimes everything comes together as it should be. It's been a great week. Joe returned from the hospital with some good news about his heart condition. I could tell it in his demeanor. His upbeat personality was constant, telling jokes and stories every time I saw him. The old salt made it to the Big Rock fishing tournament in Morehead City a couple of times this week. He made the rounds, checking out all the boats on the waterfront and listening in on the radio frequency the fishermen in the tournament used. He came back to Swansboro giving me personal accounts from the days he fished in the Big Rock tournament in the 1960s through the 1990s. The

Big Rock is a rich man's game now, costing over thirty grand for each boat to enter, and prizes of over three-million dollars are awarded.

The Billy Anna's engines also got up and running this week, the oil leak and other problems fixed by Captain Joe's mechanic and friend named Vinny. Captain Joe shared the good news with me and said that Billy Anna II was ready for another adventure. My girlfriend Melissa, my mom, Captain Joe, and I immediately made plans to take her out on a little cruise.

Good for me because I was dying to go out of the fishing vessel that assisted in helping to make Captain Joe a legend. I knew the book was coming to a close and I thought it would be symbolic to have the same four people here today as the day the idea for the book was conceived one year ago. For the last three months, I lived and breathed Swansboro. My everyday routine revolved around finding out the history of the seaside village and learning more about Captain Joe Webb.

The four of us met at Joe's Beach, the old boat rocking back and forth at high tide. I immediately knew this day was going to be one that I would remember for the rest of my life. Felt like I was in a movie, starring Captain Joe Webb and Billy Anna II. After the four of us boarded the vessel, Joe cranked the diesel engines to life one more time. They roared and rumbled, while traces of white smoke filled the air around us. From the upper tower and behind the helm, Joe yelled directions down to me, what lines to untie first. Guess today I was the captain's honorary first mate. I would be okay with that. Long as Joe was the captain, nothing could go wrong.

After all four ropes were untied from their cleats, the Billy Anna II reversed out of the pilings that surrounded her. Bystanders on nearby docks stopped what they were doing to stare at the old fishing boat going out on another voyage. Mom gave Joe some company on the tower and I held Melissa's hand as both of us stood on the stern. Once cleared from the pilings and safe from any docks, the Billy Anna II inched forward for the first time in three months. It hit me that we were leaving the very same spot Captain Otway Burns built and launched North Carolina's first steamship over two-hundred years before.

I've always loved the different perspectives you can have from the water. You see things you normally wouldn't see. One gets a sense that you wouldn't get from land. I let go of Melissa's hand, stepped to the railings on the starboard side, and took in the sights of downtown Swansboro. The quaint village began to pass by me; other berthed boats rocked back and forth from Billy Anna's wake.

Mr. Rhue popped out of the rear entrance of his antique store, waving at us. The four of us onboard waved back. Over the last few months, I've grown to like and respect the man. I could tell that he looked up to Captain Joe Webb like a big brother. The captain would consider Mr. Rhue a little brother from the conversations I've had with him. They have been friends for over seventy years and formed a special bond. Both were gray-haired men and getting long in the tooth, but both had lots of life in them.

Next, Billy Anna II passed the three-story structure of Bake Bottle and Brew, we passed Saltwater Grill, and then we came upon Poor Man's Hole. I thought about Monte Hill and Isiah Thomas and the hundreds of boats that they built in that small tidal basin. Poor Man's Hole was once a bustling part of Swansboro. All you can see now are the houses built around it and a few run-down piers. It's not much to look at any longer since the Army Corps of Engineers filled much of it with sand and oyster shells, but I could still feel the history that this place held.

Billy Anna II approached Casper's Marina. I thought about the Swansboro Land and Lumber Company that stood in that same location over a hundred years prior. I thought about the scores of men and women it once employed. I could envision smoke rising from the factory's tall smokestack. I could see tugboats towing logs up to the waterway. I also thought about the body of Jimmy Canady washing up on shore there when Joe was six years old. I thought about the Casper family and the changes the marina had been through over the last nine decades. I secretly wished W.T. Casper would come out on the docks to see us pass by. I kept my gaze on the marina, waiting for the man to appear.

*Casper's Marina*

After no luck seeing W.T. come out, my eyes went to Hawkins Creek and Deer Island. I learned about this four-acre island through Joe. It was once home to industries like a turpentine distillery and a steam-powered sawmill. Today, you only see a few aged houses sitting among old trees, scrub brush, and vegetation.

*Candy, Captain Joe and Melissa on Billy Anna II, Melissa, Captain Joe and Chad Hollamon*

With Deer Island out of view, I turned around to see Shark Tooth Island behind me. Adults sat on beach chairs and basked in the sunshine while young children searched for the much-coveted shark's teeth along the shoreline. The Billy Anna II maintained cruising speed at four knots and continued traveling down the Intracoastal Waterway. I didn't know where the captain was taking us, nor did I care. I was with three people that I loved and cared for deeply.

I felt the energy coming from those on board with me. I couldn't think of anyone I would rather be with at that time. I looked up at Mom.

I couldn't hear what Joe was saying to her, but I knew she hung on to every word the man had to say. I tightly embraced Melissa around her waist. We have had a rough few months but I love her with every fiber of my being. I was so glad she came to share this experience with me.

After Swansboro was no longer in sight behind us, I asked Melissa if she wanted to go up on deck to join the Captain and Mom. I followed Melissa up the aluminum stepladder. She took a seat on the left side of Joe, while I stood beside Mom on Joe's right side. From this height, I could see an endless chain of islands. Pictures do not do this part of the world justice. It's just one of those places you have to visit to appreciate the beauty.

I did a complete 360 to view my surroundings. I had only been through these inlets a few dozen times in my life. Captain Joe Webb had been through these channels and inlets thousands of times. I attempted to soak up every last second of this experience. I vividly remembered being in that federal prison cell for eighteen years. During that time, I could only dream about doing something like this. My eyes grew a little misty under my sunglasses and my heartstrings pulled, putting an emotional lump in my throat. I was given another chance at life and darned if I didn't get to spend this moment with the man I admired, my ever-loving mom, and the girl that I cared for immensely.

Joe proceeded to give us a little tour, telling stories like he always did. Far away on our left sat Huggin's Island. Joe pointed to where the old Civil War fort used to be. We stared in that direction, not exactly sure what we were looking at since earth embankment remnants of the fort are the only evidence it even existed. I pondered why the Confederacy chose that spot and not somewhere else. I tried to envision what the fort looked like with its numerous guns protruding out, ready for the Yankees to attack, some 150 years ago.

During one Swansboro Historical Society meeting, Ann Shuller talked about her great uncle Dan Heady Russell that once owned and lived on Huggin's Island with his wife Alice and their three children. Beginning in 1888, Dan Russell farmed and raised hogs on the island. It's even rumored that he would stay years on Huggin's Island without ever leaving. Supplies were brought to him by boat, the rest of what his family needed was self-sustained.

Dan's nephew Robert Russell purchased the 115-acre island from him in 1918. Robert's son named Mack tried to farm and raise hogs too, but he soon determined it wasn't feasible to live on the island with six children in school. Today, all 211 acres of Hugging's Island are part of Hammock's Beach.

That leads me to the Hammock's Beach ferry terminal on our right. Those same ferries carry passengers to the untouched islands on our left side. Joe pointed out where Dr. Sharpe's house used to stand. The area is now protected by the North Carolina state government, meaning it will more than likely remain full of lush vegetation and untarnished beaches for hundreds of years, allowing our descendants to see what we see today. Dr. Sharpe's efforts paid off in preserving these wetlands. As we passed Hammock's Beach, I tried to picture Dr. Sharpe and his caretaker John Hurst out for a hunt or possibly fishing together. Both would be proud of the way the Hammocks look today.

Further up the Intracoastal Waterway, we approached the Sanders property on both sides of us. You may recall a woman I got acquainted with named Gloria Sanders. Nearly 500 acres of land were passed down to her family. I'm told it was the same land the King of England granted her family over three-hundred years ago. How many families can say the King of England granted them land? Most of the 500 acres appear as they did when it was granted to them 300 years ago. For miles and miles, all you can see are various types of trees and scurrying wildlife. Captain Joe added how good the fishing was in this area. From the top deck, I wondered where my new friend Gloria was, as I admired her family's intriguing property.

Less than a half-mile later, things would get a little interesting and make me a tad nervous. Military signs began to appear that warned us not to come through when lights were flashing. This is the start of the 110,000 acres of land the federal government took over in the early 1940s. Thankfully, those signs were not flashing. This is the beginning of Camp Lejeune Marine Base. As Billy Anna II crept through the coastline, Joe reminded us that this is where the military practices dropping bombs. Bear Island they call it. No wonder our houses shake when the military practices bombing. We were in the middle of a bombing range. Miss Gloria got a front-seat view of the action if she wanted, bombs coming very close to her property. Almost felt like we were committing an illegal act. But I trusted that Joe would not bring us any harm. Still, I looked every which way for the Coast Guard or the military police coming to stop us.

*Camp LeJuene*

A mile or two later a half-sunken sailboat stuck out from the water, putting me on edge. Internally, I questioned if the military sank the civilian boat on purpose or if it accidentally ran aground. Either way, the boat appeared eerie and strange as we passed by it. Reminded me of an old movie called, 'Apocalypse Now,' starring Marlon Brando, Dennis Hopper, Harrison Ford, and Martin Sheen.

A few months before I had an interesting conversation with one of Joe's former first mates, Rob Koraly. Don't know why but I asked him what he thought should happen to Billy Anna II after Captain Joe's time on Earth. Without thinking, he suggested sinking it in a part of the Atlantic Ocean that is one of Joe's favorite fishing spots and naming the area 'Joe's Hole' or something to that effect. I didn't know what Joe's immediate family would have in store once that day came, but the former first mate's suggestion doesn't seem like a bad idea at all. That way Captain Joe's legacy would live on forever. I'd have to ask Joe his wishes. Since he asked me not to let him go to a retirement home or die in a hospital, I felt comfortable asking him about what to do with his beloved fishing vessel. He should have the final say in the matter.

Billy Anna II chugged along at a snail's pace when coming to the bridge for Onslow County Beach. Joe began turning us around and putting us back on course toward Swansboro. When we did, Melissa and I climbed back down the aluminum stepladder. Once on the stern, I straddled the gunwales portside with one leg hanging overboard in the water. With Melissa seated between my legs and me holding her, I contemplated this book as it was coming to an end. I could have written books upon books about the people I've met along my journey. All had interesting stories. Each contributed to the community of Swansboro. I hope I did their little town justice by sharing a bit of their rich history and capturing some of it in this book. My ultimate goal is for outsiders to know more about this piece of heaven. I also want the locals to know more about their heritage.

I reflected on the last three months or so. From chasing Captain Joe Webb around downtown Swansboro daily to meeting the people that know him, it's been a wonderful experience. I only scratched the surface of his colorful life, not coming close to the legend that he is. Joe lived his life his way. He didn't really care what people thought of him. He was so damn busy living his own life not worrying about what others said about his character. Guess we can all learn from him.

Captain Joe peered down at Melissa and me. He just smiled brightly and then turned back around to talk to my mom. I can see what my mom loved about him. He's caring, generous, loving, funny, and intriguing. I'm thankful she has a partner in life in Joe. He might be a lifelong bachelor, but I know he loves my mom in his way. Because of her relationship with the captain, I was able to get close to the man I came to admire and look up to.

As Melissa and I sat there in silence, except for the roar of those diesel engines, downtown Swansboro came back into view. Just like not wanting the book to end, I didn't want that boat ride to end. It was pure utopia. From this angle, downtown Swansboro has the appearance of an old fishing village up in Maine or some other northern state. Most of eastern North Carolina is flat, but for some reason, Swansboro has bluffs and ridges, unlike anything around here for hundreds of miles. Maybe that's why our forefathers originally founded this place. Maybe that's why they fought so damn hard to keep it intact. There is uniqueness and charm to this seaside village that you will not find anywhere near here.

I thought about all the historical houses in Swansboro and how efforts were made by the

Historical Society to keep them like they were. Because once one house is gone, a little bit of history goes with it. I appreciated the women I met every Thursday morning. Not only were they preserving the old look of yesteryear, they were doing what they could to keep the way of life pretty much the same until new money came in and took over. The old-school mentality like Joe has is becoming rare. Social grace like Anne Shuller is becoming a thing of the past.

I peered up at Captain Joe one more time as the boat ride was coming to a close. He sat there steering the helm with one hand, navigating his way back up to the dock from another adventure out on the water. I've been honored to be a part of this man's life. I've been blessed to spend time with one of the last legends still alive. For the rest of my life, I will repeat the stories I heard about the man and his little town of Swansboro. I will do my best to help the Historical Society preserve anything of this seaside village's past. Just as Captain Joe gave me one of my best experiences in life thirty years ago, I knew that this boat ride would bc ingrained in my consciousness until I take my last breath. Thank you, Captain Joe Webb. It's been a helluva ride.

*Legendary Captain Joe Webb and Captain Otway Burns*

## About the Author

Chad Hollamon currently splits his time up between Emerald Isle and Wilmington, North Carolina. While incarcerated in federal prison for 18 years, Chad fell in love with words and writing. After his release in 2021, he's combined writing and his passion for history. Chad adores all of Eastern North Carolina and considers it home. He's working on other books dedicated to small towns that contributed to our Nations's history as well as a sequel to Cries for Carteret.